From Hood to Hooded ™

BUILDING BEYOND BARRIERS TO LIVE UNAPOLOGETICALLY FREE

DR. SHATOYA BLACK

EDITED BY
NICOLE QUEEN

Grief has five stages that occur beyond our control, and many people do their best to push through it. However, if grief is not addressed by navigating it, talking about how we feel, and processing those emotions, it can imprison us without permission. Do not be afraid to ask for help.

To the cherished memory of my sister, who passed away on Christmas (12-25-22), and my father, who left us three weeks earlier in December 2022 (12-3-22)

You are not defined by the labels others place on you, but by the legacy you choose to create.

Contents

Introduction

Society told me I would never amount to anything. They said I'd be another number, another failure, a casualty of statistics. But here I am—a living testament that statistics do not define destiny. I am not a statistic.

This declaration became my lifeline, a bold reclamation of my journey. I refused to let my circumstances dictate my future. Growing up in a world that sought to define me by numbers and labels—poverty, fatherlessness, and the limitations of my zip code—I knew I had to blaze a new trail. This trail would not just lead to survival; it would lead to transformation, resilience, and unapologetic freedom.

Rejecting Labels & Rewriting the Narrative

The hood is a place where dreams are shaped and often shattered by the weight of societal expectations. It's a world of limited opportunities, violence, and systemic barriers. I grew up navigating these realities in a single-parent home, the eldest of six children on one side and ten on the other. My mother, a tireless provider, sacrificed to give us the basics: food, clothing, water, and shelter. Yet, even as she worked tirelessly, the world around us sent a clear message: we were less than. We were statistics.

Being the eldest meant taking on responsibilities far beyond my years—caring for my siblings, managing a household, and stepping into roles I didn't fully understand. This dynamic shaped me, but also left me grappling with feelings of inadequacy, fear, and self-doubt. Life in the projects meant watching friends and family fall victim to violence, navigating a community plagued by poverty, and being told that my potential was limited by factors beyond my control.

But even amid these challenges, I saw glimpses of hope. A village surrounded us—neighbors, teachers, and unexpected role models who encouraged resilience and perseverance. I began to understand that, while statistics aimed to box me in, I could break free.

Society's narrative for people like me was one of despair: father-less homes, poverty, and generational cycles of struggle. But I refused to let those labels define me. I chose to rewrite my story. My declaration— "I am not a statistic" —was not just a statement of defiance; it was a commitment to transformation.

This transformation was not without struggle. I wrestled with feelings of rejection and unworthiness, especially in my relation-ships. I battled generational curses and systemic barriers, deter-mined to create a life that reflected who I was meant to be—not who society said I should be. It was during this time that I found my faith, a pivotal force in my journey.

At my lowest, I found solace in God. My faith gave me the courage to break free from the limitations of my past. Through prayer and worship, I discovered a new narrative for my life—one of purpose, resilience, and freedom. I learned to see myself as God saw me: whole, capable, and destined for greatness.

This spiritual transformation helped me overcome suicidal ideations and deep-seated fears. It was in these moments that I began to envision a new framework for my life, one that would eventually become the fountain of my work helping others.

Building the Framework

The lessons I learned through my journey became the tools I now use to guide others. The *L.E.G.A.C.Y. Framework*—Leadership, Education, Growth, Advocacy, Community, and Yielding—is a model built from my lived experiences. It's not just about what we leave behind when we're gone; it's about the lives we live right now. This framework empowers people to identify where they are and what they need to move forward.

As a *Professional GPS*, I help others navigate their lives. Just as a GPS provides direction, I offer guidance, processes, and strategies for success. This work is deeply personal to me because I know what it feels like to stand at a crossroads, unsure of which path to take. I've walked this journey, and now I want to walk it with you. You don't have to navigate this alone. The same tools and principles that have guided me and countless others are here for you.

Maybe you've been told that you're not good enough. Maybe the world has tried to box you in with labels and statistics. I'm here to tell you—they lied. *You are not a statistic.* Your story is still being written, and you have the power to rewrite the narrative.

This book is a guide—a map to help you navigate life's challenges and discover the strength within you. It's a reminder that no matter where you start, you are not bound by societal expectations or the limitations of your past. You are destined for more, and together, we'll uncover the tools and strategies to help you get there.

Welcome to your journey of transformation!

Let's begin.

CHAPTER ONE
Life in the Hood

The *hood*—often misunderstood, frequently judged, but for me, it was home. It was where I learned resilience, where survival was second nature, and where dreams fought to live despite the crushing weight of societal expectations. It was a place filled with contradictions: laughter echoing from children playing jump rope outside, while the distant sound of sirens served as a constant reminder of the challenges lurking beyond the gates of our community.

Growing up in Stateway Gardens, I was no stranger to adversity. The projects, as they were called, were the epicenter of a life defined by struggle and survival. To outsiders, the hood was a place of poverty, violence, and limited potential. To those of us who lived there, it was a world of both limitations and unexpected joys—a place where community thrived even amidst hardship.

GROWING UP IN THE HOOD

Every day brought a mix of challenges and simple pleasures. I remember waking up early, getting ready for school, and sometimes sneaking in a few moments of play on the playground before the bell rang. The playground became a place of excitement and escape, where friends and I would gather before the school bell rang. We'd play games like jump rope, red light-green light, and hide-and- seek, savoring these small moments of innocence. School itself was a refuge, at times, because of the care that many of the teachers had for the students.

Ms. Vivian's presence every day after school brought a glimmer of hope and consistency, as we looked forward to seeing her. She didn't just sell penny candy, pickles, and other snacks outside her white van; she created a sense of stability and belonging in a world that often felt chaotic, and even knew us by name. The routine rhythms of the neighborhood came alive because we understood the concept of being a village.

During the summer, friends would knock on our door, asking, "Are you coming down for chokes?"— our slang for the free meals provided by the government program. My siblings and I would head downstairs to eat, then return outside to play basketball, hang out on the porch, or sit on the stump near our building, talking about anything and everything. Sometimes, we'd simply enjoy the freedom of being kids, running, laughing, and finding joy in the simplest activities. Those meals, though simple, represented moments of connection and shared community.

Saturday mornings brought a different kind of routine; they were dedicated to cleaning. My mom's favorite old-school music would fill our home as we scrubbed floors, organized our rooms, and prepared for the weekend. Despite the hard work, there was a sense of connection during those mornings. Her voice, singing along to the music, carried both a sense of pride and a weight of exhaustion as a single mother.

At night, there were times we would turn our porch into a makeshift movie theater. My siblings and I would drag mattresses outside, set up the television, and watch movies under the stars. With popcorn in hand and blankets spread out, those evenings felt like magic. It was a rare moment of peace and unity, surrounded by the people I loved most. Other times, we would bring speakers onto the porch to play music so people could come over to hang out and dance because my mom made it very clear that we were not allowed to leave the porch.

Despite the moments of joy, life in the hood was not easy. Poverty was a constant reality, shaping every aspect of our lives. My mother worked tirelessly to provide for us, but the weight of raising six children on her own often left her frustrated and overwhelmed. The anger she carried sometimes spilled over into our household, manifesting in yelling or harsh punishments. Looking back, I understand that her struggles weren't just about us being "bad." They were the result of her own pain, compounded by a system that offered little support and by fathers who were absent— failing to provide financial, physical, or emotional support to share the burden of parenthood.

Violence was another shadow that loomed over our community. While we created our own sense of safety within our tight-knit neighborhood, the larger world was unpredictable. There were drive-bys, gang rivalries, and encounters with the police that left everyone on edge. My mother would call us inside as soon as the streetlights came on, shouting from the porch to make sure we were safe. Her voice was a lifeline, pulling us out of harm's way even as she faced her own battles.

The emotional weight of growing up in the hood was heavy. As the eldest child, I bore responsibilities far beyond my years. I helped my siblings with their homework, ensured they were fed, and often acted as a second parent. My childhood was a delicate balance of innocence and responsibility, of dreaming about the future while navigating the harsh realities of the present. The hood gave me community and connection, but it couldn't shield me from the emotional battles I faced at home. There were deeper wounds that I carried—wounds that stemmed from the relationship with my father— a bond that was as complex as it was distant.

A COMPLEX RELATIONSHIP WITH MY FATHER

Amidst these challenges, my relationship with my father added another layer of complexity. He wasn't present in the ways I needed him to be, and yet I longed for his love and approval. I would watch from our porch, scanning the street for his car, my heart leaping whenever I caught a glimpse of him driving by. Those moments, fleeting as they were, felt like promises of connection and care. I would run to meet him, hoping that this time, he'd stay a little longer, that this time, I'd feel like I mattered to him.

But the moments were always brief. He would stop for a while, perhaps exchange a few words, and then he was gone again, disappearing just as quickly as he'd arrived. Even as a child, I could sense the weight he carried—the burden of his own unresolved pain and the distance he placed between himself and those who loved him. Still, I chased him, both literally and figuratively, holding onto the hope that one day he would see me as worthy of his time and affection.

He often apologized, but his words were heavy with regret rather than resolution. "I don't know how to love," he would tell me. "I never learned. No one loved me." As a child, I couldn't understand how someone could not know how to love their own child or be the example of what they desire to have. His words left me confused and hurt, but they also planted seeds of curiosity. Why couldn't he love me? What was it that he was missing?

As I grew older, I began to piece together the story of his life—a story marked by abandonment, trauma, and generational pain. My father spoke of his own mother, the physical and emotional abuse he endured at her hands and the resentment he carried because of it. He described being beaten, cursed at, and ultimately sent away to live with his grandmother and great-grandmother. His words painted a picture of a boy who never felt wanted, who learned early on that survival often came at the cost of emotional connection.

But even as I began to understand his struggles, the hurt didn't disappear. His rejection was a wound that time couldn't easily heal. It wasn't just the absence of his presence; it was the absence of his belief in me. It felt as though no matter how much I tried to show him love, it was never enough to bridge the gap between us. The more I sought his attention, the more distant he became. It felt as though he was running from something, but I was determined to love him unconditionally and remind him that, although he wasn't there early on, he could be present for me now because I needed him to help fill the void.

When I visited him, the dynamic was always the same. He would be there, often preoccupied with his own life. I would sit in another room with my siblings, waiting for him to acknowledge me. Even small gestures, like bringing food, felt transactional—he would hand it over and retreat into his own space, leaving me to wonder why I couldn't be the center of his attention, even for a little while. I held onto the few things he gave me, cherishing them as though they were treasures, because I knew they might be all I'd get.

There were moments when he would open up, sharing pieces of his heart that he rarely showed anyone else. He would tell me about my mother—the only woman he ever truly loved, according to him —and how their relationship ended. I came to realize that his feelings for her, unresolved and filled with resentment, may have spilled over into the way he treated me. I was a living reminder of a love that had failed, and perhaps that was a burden he couldn't bear.

Despite everything, I loved him fiercely. I didn't know how to stop. I saw his flaws, his pain, and his shortcomings, but I also saw glimpses of the man he could have been. I wanted to believe that he could change, that he could learn to love me the way I needed him to. But as much as I hoped for that day, I also learned to stop waiting for it.

The complexity of our relationship shaped me in ways I'm still discovering. It taught me about longing, about the ways we seek validation from those who may never give it. It showed me the power of forgiveness—not because someone deserves it, but because it frees you from the weight of carrying their pain. And most importantly, it taught me that my worth is not defined by someone else's ability to see it.

Looking back, I see my father for who he was—a man shaped by his own brokenness, doing the best he could with what he had. I still carry the lessons of our relationship, but I no longer carry the burden of believing that his inability to love was a reflection of my worth. It wasn't. It never was. Now that he has passed away, I want to always be reminded of his lived legacy—the effort he put into changing his life for the better and the many lives he impacted after giving his life to Christ, as well.

SEEDS OF TRANSFORMATION

While my relationship with my father left its mark, it didn't define me. In the midst of the emotional weight I carried, life in the hood presented moments of possibility—glimmers of a future where I could rise above the limitations of my circumstances. These seeds of transformation, though small at first, began to take root as I sought out opportunities that offered a glimpse of a world beyond what I had known. These moments didn't come from the circumstances around me, but from the opportunities I seized, often hidden in plain sight. Community programs, summer jobs, and leadership initiatives became my windows to a world I had only dared to imagine.

Growing up, the hood felt like it was the entire world—a place where every experience, every struggle, and every triumph was contained within its boundaries, shaping how we understood life and what we believed was possible. The same streets, the same faces, the same routines defined our daily lives. But every now and then, something new would break through the monotony. A local banker leading a community workshop, a summer camp program offering leadership training, or a church initiative inviting young people to explore their potential—these weren't programs; they were lifelines for me.

I was always the first to volunteer for these experiences. While many of my peers hesitated, uncertain about leaving the familiar confines of our neighborhood, I felt a deep pull to explore. Something in me yearned to know what existed beyond the invisible boundaries of the hood. These opportunities weren't just events on a calendar; they were acts of rebellion against the limitations that society and circumstances had placed on us.

Summer jobs were more than a way to earn a little money—they became classrooms for life. I worked at local summer camps and community centers, places where mentors modeled the kind of leadership that inspired change. They didn't just tell me to dream bigger; they showed me how. They treated me not as a statistic or a charity case, but as someone with potential, someone worth investing in.

These mentors taught me the value of hard work and responsibility. They showed me that leadership wasn't about standing above others; it was about lifting them up. I watched as they poured their hearts into creating opportunities for kids like me, and I began to believe that I could one day do the same. The seeds of transformation were planted in these moments—not through grand gestures, but through the consistent, quiet belief that I could be more than the circumstances I was born into.

For many in the hood, stepping outside our community felt like stepping into the unknown. The world beyond seemed vast and unwelcoming, a place where we didn't belong. But I was determined to push those boundaries. Whether it was attending a leadership workshop, participating in a community meeting, or taking on responsibilities that scared me, I embraced every chance to step beyond my comfort zone.

These experiences opened my eyes to the possibilities that existed beyond survival. I began to imagine a life where I could thrive. I started to see myself not just as a participant in these programs, but as a leader who could create them. It wasn't just about seeing a different world; it was about seeing myself differently. I realized that I didn't have to accept the limits placed on me by others—I could define my own potential.

OVERCOMING LABELS AND EXPECTATIONS

Society's labels weighed heavily on us, pressing down like an invisible weight that seemed impossible to shake. Poverty. Violence. Fatherlessness. These words weren't just descriptors; they were judgments—assumptions that painted our futures before we even had a chance to dream for ourselves. To many outsiders, we were nothing more than statistics, products of a broken system destined to fail. Teachers, community leaders, and even well-meaning programs often reinforced these low expectations, using statistics as the basis to predict who we were and what we could achieve. It felt as though the mere fact of where we lived—our zip code—had already determined our destiny.

This narrative didn't just exist in words; it showed up in how we were treated. Teachers sometimes spoke to us as if we were incapable of achieving greatness, as though our environment had already sealed our fate. Community programs, while often helpful, sometimes operated under the assumption that our success would always be limited by the confines of the hood. The subtle message was clear: we weren't expected to do more than survive.

But even as a child, something in me resisted those labels. I refused to let them define me. I knew I wanted something more, even if I couldn't yet articulate what "more" looked like. While many of my peers gave in to the temptations of our environment—drinking, smoking, or making choices that led to dead ends—I made decisions that set me apart. It wasn't because I thought I was better than anyone else. It was because I felt a pull toward a different path, one that I couldn't yet see, but knew existed.

For me, it wasn't just about saying "no" to certain behaviors; it was about preserving my ability to dream. I wanted to keep my mind clear and my heart open to the possibilities that lay beyond the hood. I believed, even in the face of overwhelming doubt from those around me, that I could create a different life. The statistics said I was more likely to drop out of school than graduate, more likely to end up in poverty than to rise above it. They said children from fatherless homes were destined to repeat cycles of abandonment and struggle. They said that violence and poverty would define my relationships, my opportunities, and my sense of self. But I knew that statistics were not destiny—they were patterns, and patterns could be broken.

I made choices that reflected this belief. I avoided the traps that seemed to ensnare so many, not because it was easy, but because I was determined to prove the world wrong. I wanted to show that our environment didn't have to dictate our future. I wanted to be an example, not just for myself, but for those around me, that it was possible to rise above the expectations placed upon us.

Even as I resisted the labels and judgments, I still faced the challenge of figuring out what "more" actually meant. Growing up in the hood, it was hard to dream of something you'd never seen. The world outside our neighborhood felt distant and unreachable, like an entirely different universe. Everyone didn't have examples of upward mobility, of people who had made it out and come back to show us how. Dreaming of a better life required imagination, hope, and a defiant belief in possibilities that seemed impossible.

I didn't know where my choices would lead me, but I knew I didn't want to stay trapped by the labels others had assigned to me. I dreamed of a life where I wasn't just surviving, but thriving. I didn't yet have the roadmap, but I had the will to forge my own path. The more I resisted the labels, the clearer it became to me that transformation wasn't just about escaping the hood—it was about rejecting the limitations placed on me and daring to believe in something greater.

Every decision I made—every time I chose to study instead of giving in to distractions, every time I chose to avoid behaviors that could derail my future—was a small act of rebellion against the narrative society had written for me. Each choice was a step toward rewriting my own story, a story where I was not defined by poverty, violence, or fatherlessness, but by resilience, courage, and hope.

Overcoming labels and expectations wasn't a single moment or act; it was a daily commitment to seeing myself differently and daring to believe in a life I had never known. It was a journey of faith, persistence, and an unwavering refusal to let others define my worth. I was determined to break generational curses so took the path of becoming a cycle breaker.

A BADGE OF HONOR

To outsiders, life in the hood might seem like something to escape, something to bury in the past and never look back on. For many, it's a symbol of struggle, hardship, and a life marked by limitations. But for me, the hood became a badge of honor. It wasn't just the back-drop of my life—it was the crucible that forged my resilience, the furnace where my grit was tested and strengthened. It was a place that taught me lessons I carry to this day, lessons about the power of community, survival, street smarts, and finding hope in the unlike-liest places.

The hood didn't just test me; it prepared me. Every challenge, every obstacle, every stereotype, betrayal, I overcame became part of the foundation for the person I would become. Life in the hood wasn't just about survival—it was about learning how to thrive in the face of adversity. It was where I learned to dream beyond my circumstances, even when those dreams felt impossibly far away.

The hood was a crucible, a place where adversity wasn't the exception, but the norm. From the constant weight of systemic oppression to the day-to-day struggles of living in poverty, every aspect of life in the hood demanded strength and perseverance. There were moments that tested me to my core—whether it was navigating the emotional strain of broken relationships, witnessing violence that left scars on my heart, or simply trying to keep my family together while still being a child myself. But each of these experiences became a part of my story, not as wounds, but as proof of my ability to endure.

Resilience wasn't optional; it was a necessity. When resources were scarce, we found ways to make do. When violence loomed, we leaned on our community for protection and comfort. And when the world outside seemed determined to box us in with labels and expectations, we found ways to push back. The hood taught me that resilience is way more than simply surviving; it's about growing stronger, about finding the courage to dream in the face of obstacles and the determination to turn those dreams into reality.

The hood also taught me the importance of community. In a world where resources were limited, we relied on each other. Neighbors became extended family, stepping in to fill the gaps left by absent parents, financial struggles, or the daily grind of survival. The phrase "it takes a village" wasn't just a saying—it was a way of life.

I'll never forget the moments when the community came together, whether it was sharing food, supporting each other through losses, or simply creating safe spaces for kids to play and dream. Even in the midst of hardship, there was a spirit of togetherness that I've rarely seen elsewhere. The hood showed me that strength doesn't always come from individual effort; sometimes, it's the collective power of people who care for each other that makes the greatest impact.

For many, the hood is a place to leave behind, a chapter to close. But for me, it was the starting point of my transformation. The lessons I learned there didn't just shape me; they prepared me for the journey ahead. They taught me that while the world might see the hood as a place of failure, it was, for me, a place of potential. It was where I began to see that the circumstances you're born into don't have to dictate the life you build for yourself.

Living in the hood wasn't just about enduring adversity; it was about finding the strength to rewrite the narrative. It was about realizing that the labels and limitations others placed on me didn't have to define me. The hood wasn't just where I came from—it was where I found the courage to dream bigger, to imagine a life where I could not only survive, but thrive.

The hood planted the seeds of change, setting me on a path that would eventually lead from hood to hooded™. The grit and resilience I developed there became the foundation for my transformation, propelling me toward opportunities I hadn't even imagined. The hood didn't just give me stories to tell; it gave me the strength to tell them. It gave me the determination to rise above, not by denying where I came from, but by embracing it as a part of who I am.

Today, I carry the lessons of the hood with me as a badge of honor. It's not a symbol of shame or regret—it's a testimony of the strength, courage, and hope that were forged in the crucible of my early life. The hood taught me that no matter where you start, you have the power to rewrite your story. And for that, I am forever grateful. Though I didn't know it then, the grit and resilience I developed in the hood were preparing me for a journey I couldn't yet envision —a journey that would eventually take me from hood to hooded™.

SELF-AWARENESS & REFLECTION

1. Childhood Memories: Reflect on a defining moment from your childhood that taught you resilience or shaped your outlook on life. What did you learn from that experience?

_____
_____
_____
_____
_____
_____
_____
_____
_____
_____
_____
_____

2. Community Strength: Think of a time when your community came together to support one another. How did it impact your sense of belonging and hope?

_____
_____
_____
_____
_____
_____
_____
_____
_____
_____
_____
_____

3. Complex Relationships: Explore a relationship in your life that was both painful and transformative. How has it influenced the person you are today?

_____

_____

_____

_____

_____

_____

_____

_____

_____

_____

4. Overcoming Labels: What labels or expectations have others placed on you that you've worked to defy? How have you rewritten the narrative for yourself?

_____

_____

_____

_____

_____

_____

_____

_____

_____

_____

_____

_____

_____

5. Sources of Resilience: What external or internal resources have helped you navigate challenges in your life? How can you continue to draw strength from them?

_____

_____

_____

_____

_____

_____

_____

_____

_____

_____

_____

_____

TIPS FOR NAVIGATING LIFE'S CHALLENGES

- *Find Joy in Small Moments:* Even in difficult circumstances, seek out simple pleasures and moments of connection that can uplift your spirit.

- *Build Your Village*: Surround yourself with a community of people who support, uplift, and inspire you. Resilience often grows through shared strength.

- *Embrace Dualities:* Life is often a mix of joy and hardship. Recognize and honor both aspects to create a balanced perspective.

- *Resist Labels:* Define yourself on your own terms, rather than accepting the labels others assign to you.

- *Carry Lessons Forward*: Reflect on how your past experiences have prepared you for future opportunities. Every challenge carries a lesson that can propel you forward.

How can you implement the aforementioned tips in your daily life?

_____

_____

_____

_____

_____

_____

_____

_____

_____

_____

_____

_____

QUOTES TO INSPIRE

Do not judge me by my success; judge me by how many times I fell down and got back up again.
— *Nelson Mandela*

You are not entitled to anything, but deserve everything. You have many choices, but defeat is not an option.
— *Dr. Shatoya Black*

It takes a village to raise a child. — *African Proverb*

After reflecting on these quotes, journal your thoughts below.

_____
_____
_____
_____
_____
_____
_____
_____
_____
_____
_____
_____
_____
_____
_____
_____
_____
_____
_____
_____
_____
_____
_____
_____
_____
_____
_____
_____
_____
_____

CHAPTER TWO

Matters of the Heart

T he heart is the compass of our lives. It guides our decisions, shapes our emotions, and serves as the vessel for both our pain and our hope. But what happens when that compass is broken? When the weight of disappointment, rejection, and unfulfilled promises clouds the path forward? Matters of the heart are more than love or relationships; they are about survival, healing, and transformation. For me, understanding the matters of my heart was the first step toward becoming whole.

THE WEIGHT OF DEFERRED HOPE

The Bible says, "Hope deferred makes the heart sick," and I lived this truth every day. The absence of hope is a sickness that festers in the soul, an unrelenting ache that shapes how you see the world and your place in it. Deferred hope does more than disappoint; it overwhelms, turning dreams into burdens and possibilities into impossibilities. Chronic disappointment compounds this weight, transforming hope into hopelessness, and hopelessness into despair. Each broken promise, each moment of feeling unseen and unheard, added another layer of heaviness to my heart.

Growing up, I carried the burden of deferred hope like a constant shadow. It was in the silent spaces between what I longed for and what I received. I hoped for love from my father, love that never came in the way I needed. I hoped for stability in a world that often felt chaotic and unpredictable. I hoped for safety, for a home where I felt secure. And I hoped, above all, for a sense of belonging—a place where I wasn't just tolerated, but cherished. Each unmet expectation chipped away at my belief in myself, in others, and in the idea that life could ever be different.

Deferred hope seeps into your thoughts, behaviors, and relationships. It manifests as self-doubt, anger, or a desperate need to prove yourself. For me, it showed up as an internal war: a relentless fight against feelings of inadequacy, even as I clung to the idea that something better had to be possible. But when you don't understand the depths of your wounds, how can you begin to heal? When you don't even have the language to articulate your pain, how can you expect to move past it?

This weight shaped how I interacted with the world. I found myself overcompensating, trying to prove that I was enough—even if I didn't fully believe it myself. I would excel in school, in responsibilities, and in helping others, hoping that my efforts would fill the void left by all the ways I felt unseen. But the harder I tried, the more it seemed like the gap widened. I was trying to prove something to others, while also trying to prove something to myself— that I mattered, that my existence held value.

The absence of hope is like an invisible chain. It keeps you tethered to the very thing you're trying to escape. It makes you believe that reaching for more is futile, that dreaming of better is an act of naivety. I didn't just feel like I was failing; I felt like I was failing myself, my family, and even the idea of who I was meant to be. It's a cruel paradox—knowing you want more, but feeling powerless to achieve it.

Looking back, I see how deeply this deferred hope was tied to my circumstances. In the hood, dreaming big was seen as unrealistic. We were taught, subtly and overtly, to accept the limitations placed on us. Whether it was the lack of resources in our schools or the scarcity of opportunities in our community, everything around us seemed to whisper that hope was a luxury we couldn't afford. This message wasn't always spoken; sometimes, it was just in the way people looked at us or the dismissive tone they used when speaking about our futures.

Deferred hope isn't just a product of external circumstances—it's also internal. It lives in the way you talk to yourself, the stories you tell yourself about who you are and what you deserve. I told myself that I was too much and not enough all at once. Too much anger, too much need, too much emotion—but not enough strength, not enough talent, not enough worth. This narrative became a loop in my mind, replaying every time I faced another disappointment. It became the lens through which I saw myself and my place in the world.

One of the hardest parts of carrying deferred hope is the isolation it creates. When you feel like your dreams are unattainable, it's easy to pull back from others. You don't want to burden them with your pain, and you don't want to admit just how much you're struggling. So, you put on a brave face, pretending that everything is fine, even as your heart feels like it's breaking. This isolation only deepens the cycle, making it harder to reach out, to trust, or to believe that things could ever change.

But even in the midst of all this despair, there was a small part of me that refused to let go of hope entirely. It was faint, like a flickering candle in a dark room, but it was there. This tiny spark whispered that better was possible, even if I couldn't see how. It told me to keep going, to keep dreaming, even when the world told me to stop. It wasn't loud or insistent; it was quiet, almost imperceptible. But it was enough.

Deferred hope is a heavy weight, but it is not an unmovable one. It takes courage to confront it, to name it, and to begin the work of healing. For me, that journey started with acknowledging the pain I

I carried and giving myself permission to feel it. It started with under-standing that my worth wasn't defined by my circumstances or by the people who had failed to see me. And it started with a choice—a choice to believe that, no matter how heavy the weight felt, I could find a way to set it down.

That choice didn't come easily, and it didn't come quickly. But it came. And with it, the first glimmers of transformation began to take root. It was the beginning of a journey—a journey to reclaim hope, to rewrite my story, and to heal the matters of my heart.

GENERATIONAL WOUNDS

As I began to examine the state of my heart, I came to a difficult real-ization: much of my pain wasn't entirely mine. It was inherited, passed down like an unwanted family heirloom from one generation to the next. I wasn't just carrying the weight of my own experiences —I was carrying the weight of my family's history, their struggles, their pain, and their unspoken wounds. The trauma that shaped my father, the frustrations that molded my mother, the unaddressed grief that lingered in the corners of our family's story—they all found their way to me.

My father's life was marked by scars he never truly healed from. His childhood, steeped in abuse and neglect, left him with an anger he couldn't explain and a love he struggled to express. He spoke of being beaten by his mother, of being sent away to live with his grandmother and great-grandmother, and of a life defined by rejec-tion. He would apologize to me, saying he didn't know how to love because he had never been loved. As a child, his words left me confused, but as I grew older, I began to understand the generational wounds that shaped him. His pain wasn't just a part of his story—it was now a part of mine.

My mother, though a source of strength in many ways, also carried her own set of traumas. Her life was filled with challenges that no one should have to face alone. As a single mother, navigating

poverty, raising six children, and dealing with the absence of consistent support, her frustrations often spilled over into our home. She
did her best to provide and protect us, but the weight she bore sometimes translated into anger and harshness. Her struggle to maintain
control in a world that felt uncontrollable left little room for vulnerability or emotional expression. The result was a home where love
existed, but so did unspoken pain.

Generational trauma is a silent thief. It sneaks into your life
unnoticed, influencing your reactions, your fears, and your choices.
The anger I carried wasn't just mine—it was my father's anger, my
mother's anger, the frustration and hopelessness of ancestors who
had lived and endured in a world that often denied them dignity. The
hyper-vigilance that kept me safe in the hood, always watching for
danger, also kept me from fully trusting others. The belief that I had
to do everything on my own wasn't resilience; it was a survival
mechanism born out of watching my mother navigate life without
the support she deserved. These patterns, these beliefs, were not
uniquely mine—they were generational curses handed down
through generations.

Acknowledging these wounds was excruciating. It meant
confronting the ways I had been shaped by forces outside my
control. It meant revisiting memories of moments when I felt abandoned, misunderstood, or unsafe. It meant recognizing the ways in
which my family's pain had seeped into my own sense of identity. I
began to see how the patterns of the past influenced my present—
how my father's emotional unavailability mirrored my struggle to
open up to others, how my mother's need for control mirrored my
own attempts to micromanage my life out of fear.

But acknowledgment is the first step to healing. As painful as it
was to confront these generational wounds, it also gave me clarity. I
began to understand that while these patterns had shaped me, they
didn't have to define me. Generational trauma may run deep, but it is
not unchangeable. We inherit pain, but we also inherit the strength
to confront it. The cycles that perpetuate suffering can be broken,

but doing so requires intention, courage, and a commitment to something better.

Breaking the cycle wasn't just about recognizing the trauma—it was about actively choosing to respond differently. I had to unlearn the patterns that had been ingrained in me since childhood. I had to teach myself to trust, even when my instinct was to protect myself at all costs. I had to learn to be vulnerable, even when I feared rejection. And most importantly, I had to redefine what love looked like—not just love for others, but love for myself.

Healing generational wounds is not a straightforward path. It's a journey filled with setbacks and revelations, with moments of clarity and moments of doubt. But it's also a journey of empowerment. Each step I took toward healing was a step away from the pain that had been passed down to me. Each decision to break a pattern, to address a fear, to nurture a relationship, was a declaration that the cycle stopped with me.

I realized that healing wasn't just for me—it was for the generations that would come after me and those that looked up to me. By doing the hard work of confronting these wounds, I was creating a foundation of strength, resilience, and love for the future. I was ensuring that the pain of the past wouldn't dictate the possibilities of tomorrow.

Generational trauma thrives in silence, in avoidance, and in denial. Healing begins with acknowledgment, with giving voice to the pain and deciding that it will no longer have power over you. It begins when we recognize that the wounds we carry are not solely our own, but that we have the power to heal them, for ourselves and for those who come after us. That choice—to confront, to heal, to grow—is where the cycle breaks and where freedom begins.

THE ROLE OF FAITH

My journey toward healing would have been impossible without faith. It became the compass that guided me through the darkest moments of my life. Growing up amidst the chaos and challenges of the hood, faith was not always an obvious presence. But as I began to grapple with the weight of my past and the generational wounds I carried, my relationship with God became a transformative force in my life. It was through this relationship that I began to understand the true nature of love, the depth of forgiveness, and the possibility of renewal.

The unconditional love of Christ became the model for the love I longed to embody—not just for others, but for myself. I had spent so much of my life believing that love was conditional, that it had to be earned or deserved. My father's inability to love me the way I needed, the societal judgment placed on kids like me, the constant pressure to prove myself—all of it had ingrained in me the belief that love was a transaction, something given only if you met the right conditions. But God's love turned that narrative on its head. It was a love that didn't require perfection, a love that met me exactly where I was, in all my brokenness and pain.

Faith taught me that I didn't have to be defined by my past. I didn't have to live in anger or bitterness, even though I had every reason to. God's love revealed the places in my heart that were fractured—the rejection, the hopelessness, the self-harm, the wounds passed down from my family—and offered me the strength to begin mending them. This wasn't an overnight transformation; it was a daily process of surrendering my pain, my fears, and my doubts to God. Each day brought its own challenges, but it also brought new opportunities for healing and growth.

Through prayer, I found a safe space to pour out the emotions I had suppressed for so long. The anger I carried toward my father, the hurt I felt from being misunderstood, the fear of not being enough—all of it came pouring out in those quiet moments with God. Prayer was a lifeline, a moment of vulnerability where I could lay everything at His feet without fear of judgment. It was through these moments that I began to feel lighter, as though the burdens I had carried alone for so long were finally being shared.

Reflection played an equally important role. Faith allowed me to step back and view my journey from a new perspective. I began to see the beauty in the struggle, the purpose in the pain. I realized that every experience—no matter how painful—had shaped me in ways that were ultimately for my good. Growth often comes with pain, and healing requires us to confront the very things we've been avoiding. Faith didn't erase my struggles, but it gave me the courage to face them head-on, knowing I wasn't alone.

One of the most profound lessons faith taught me was the power of forgiveness. I had every reason to hold on to anger—toward my father for his absence, toward society for its judgment, and even toward myself for the mistakes I made along the way. But God's love showed me that forgiveness wasn't about letting others off the hook; it was about freeing myself from the chains of bitterness and resentment. Forgiveness wasn't easy, but it was necessary. Each time I chose to forgive, I felt a piece of the weight I had been carrying fall away. It was as if God was gently reminding me that holding on to pain would only keep me from the fullness of life he had planned for me.

Faith also redefined what strength meant to me. Growing up, strength had always been about endurance—about surviving, pushing through, and never showing weakness. But God showed me that true strength lies in vulnerability, in admitting when you're hurt, in asking for help, and in allowing yourself to be loved. This was perhaps the hardest lesson for me to learn, but it was also the most liberating. I didn't have to carry everything on my own. I didn't have to be perfect or invulnerable. God's strength was made perfect in my weakness, and in Him, I found a safe place to rest.

Through faith, I began to rebuild my identity. I was no longer defined by my circumstances, my past, or the labels others had placed on me. I was defined by who God said I was—loved, chosen, worthy, courageous, and capable of transformation. This realization didn't just change the way I saw myself; it changed the way I approached life. I no longer felt the need to prove my worth to others or to strive for validation. I could stand confidently in the truth of who I was, knowing that my value was intrinsic and unshakable.

Faith became the foundation for every step of my healing jour-ney. It gave me the courage to confront the parts of myself I had avoided, the grace to forgive those who had hurt me, and the strength to dream of a future that looked nothing like my past. It was through faith that I learned to love unconditionally, to embrace vulnerability, and to trust that even in the midst of pain, God was working all things together for my good.

Today, I carry the lessons of faith with me as a guiding light. It reminds me that healing is a journey, not a destination, and that every step—no matter how small—is a step toward wholeness. It reminds me that I am not defined by my wounds, but by the resilience and hope that have grown in their place. And most impor-tantly, it reminds me that I am never walking this journey alone.

EMOTIONAL AWAKENING

One of the most transformative lessons I learned during this journey was the immense value of emotional intelligence. For so much of my life, I believed that emotions were a weakness—something to suppress, ignore, or push aside in favor of survival. Expressing vulnerability, I thought, would only make me more susceptible to pain or rejection. But what I didn't realize was that suppressing emotions doesn't make them disappear; it only turns them inward, creating an internal war that manifests in ways you can't always control—anger, depression, self-doubt, lack of identity, or even a deep sense of isolation.

Emotional intelligence, I came to learn, is about much more than understanding your emotions. It's about managing them in a way that fosters growth and connection, while also acknowledging and respecting the emotions of others. Developing this skill was not easy, especially because I had spent years internalizing messages that told me my feelings or voice didn't matter. The process began with self-awareness—a painfully honest look at myself and the emotions I had worked so hard to suppress. It was uncomfortable and often overwhelming, but it was necessary. For the first time, I gave myself permission to feel everything: sadness, anger, disappointment, fear, and even joy. I began to understand that feeling an emotion didn't mean it had to define me; it was simply a part of my human experience.

Self-awareness became the foundation for everything else. I had to face the parts of myself that I didn't want to acknowledge—the resentment I carried toward people who had hurt me, the fear of rejection that kept me from forming deeper connections, and the guilt I felt for wanting something more than the life I had known. These emotions were not pleasant to confront, but they were a necessary starting point. I began to see them not as obstacles, but as signals, guiding me toward the areas of my life that needed attention and healing.

This awakening was also about the way I navigated relationships. I realized that I had spent so much of my life as a people pleaser, trying to keep the peace, avoid conflict, and meet everyone else's needs at the expense of my own. I thought this was the best way to maintain relationships, but in reality, it left me feeling drained, unappreciated, and often resentful. These patterns weren't sustainable, and they certainly weren't healthy.

True emotional intelligence required a radical shift in how I viewed and approached relationships. It meant setting boundaries—something I had never felt empowered to do before. I had to learn that saying "no" wasn't an act of rejection, but a necessary act of self-preservation. I had to unlearn the belief that advocating for my own needs was selfish or that it would push people away. In fact, I found that the more I respected my own boundaries, the more I attracted relationships built on mutual respect and understanding.

Setting boundaries didn't come without its challenges. It forced me to confront the fear of losing people who were important to me. I worried that speaking up for myself or prioritizing my own needs would make others see me as difficult or unworthy of their time. But as I began to practice, I realized that the people who truly cared for me didn't leave—they adapted. They respected the new version of me that was emerging, one who no longer hid behind a mask of compliance or sacrificed her own well-being to make others comfortable.

Another crucial aspect of emotional intelligence was learning to navigate conflict in a healthier way. For years, I avoided conflict at all costs, thinking it would preserve relationships. But this avoidance often led to unresolved issues, simmering resentment, and a lack of authenticity in my interactions. I had to reframe my perspective on conflict, seeing it not as a threat, but as an opportunity for growth and understanding. Learning to communicate openly and assertively allowed me to express my needs and concerns without fear of rejection or judgment.

Perhaps the most liberating part of my emotional awakening was letting go of the need for control. I had spent so much of my life trying to manage every aspect of my relationships and interactions, fearing that if I didn't, everything would fall apart. But emotional intelligence taught me that I couldn't control how others felt or reacted—I could only control my own actions and responses. This realization lifted a tremendous weight off my shoulders. It allowed me to show up authentically in my relationships, without the constant pressure to manage everyone else's emotions.

Through this journey, I also discovered the importance of empathy—not just for others, but for myself. I had been so hard on myself for so long, holding myself to impossible standards and berating myself for any perceived failure. Emotional intelligence taught me to extend the same compassion to myself that I so freely gave to others. I learned to recognize my own humanity, to forgive myself for mistakes, and to celebrate my progress, no matter how small it seemed.

This process of awakening wasn't linear. There were moments when I fell back into old patterns, moments when the weight of my emotions felt too heavy to bear. But each time, I reminded myself that growth is a journey, not a destination. The more I practiced self-awareness, self-regulation, and empathy, the stronger my emotional resilience became. I began to see my emotions not as something to fear, but as valuable tools for understanding myself and the world around me.

Today, emotional intelligence is a cornerstone of how I live and connect with others. It has transformed the way I view myself, my relationships, and the challenges I face. It has given me the courage to be vulnerable, the strength to set boundaries, and the wisdom to navigate life with grace and authenticity. Most importantly, it has taught me that true strength lies not in suppressing your emotions, but in understanding and embracing them. Through this awakening, I found a deeper sense of peace, purpose, and connection—a foundation that continues to support me on my journey of transformation.

THE EMOTIONAL WEIGHT OF CHANGE

Deciding to confront the matters of my heart was, without question, one of the hardest things I have ever done. Change carries an emotional weight, heavier than I could have imagined. It demands that you look honestly at yourself, peeling back the layers of behaviors and beliefs that have defined you for years, even decades. It forces you to confront uncomfortable truths, unearth buried pain, and reconcile with the parts of yourself you've long ignored or hidden. Change is a relentless process, one that challenges your endurance, your courage, and your willingness to let go of who you were to become who you're meant to be.

The weight of change lies not only in the work it requires, but in the isolation it often brings. As I faithfully endured my journey of transformation, I found myself distanced from some of the people I loved most. Change has a way of making others uncomfortable, especially those who are unwilling or unable to face their own pain. My growth re!ected truths they weren't ready to see, and it created a

divide I hadn't anticipated. The very people I thought would celebrate my progress sometimes viewed it as a threat. Their discomfort
became a new source of loneliness, a reminder that transformation
often comes at a cost.

But as difficult as it was, choosing to change was also deeply
liberating. For the first time, I felt a sense of agency over my own life
—a belief that I could shape my destiny instead of being a perpetual
victim of my circumstances. It was empowering to realize that I
didn't have to be defined by my past or by the pain that had been
handed down to me. Change wasn't about erasing the past or
pretending it hadn't happened; change was about finding meaning
in it, about using it as a foundation for growth. My struggles were no
longer weights that held me back; they became stepping stones that
propelled me forward.

The process of change demanded that I unlearn many of the
survival mechanisms I had relied on for years. These mechanisms—
people-pleasing, suppressing my emotions, avoiding conflict—had
served their purpose in helping me navigate a challenging environment, but they no longer served the person I wanted to become.
Unlearning them was both painful and disorienting. It felt like
tearing down a house while still living inside it. But with each
dismantled habit or belief, I created space for something new:
healthier patterns, deeper self-awareness, and a more authentic way
of being.

Healing, I discovered, isn't about perfection. It's not a straight
process with a clear endpoint. It's messy and zigzagged, filled with
setbacks and moments of doubt. There were times when the weight
of change felt unbearable, and I questioned whether it was worth the
effort. But those moments taught me resilience. They reminded me
that growth often feels like breaking before it feels like building.

As I began to heal, I noticed changes not just in myself, but in the
people around me including my daughter. My transformation
created a ripple effect, challenging those closest to me to confront
their own pain and patterns. Some embraced this challenge, finding

inspiration in my journey to start their own. Others resisted, clinging to the familiar and viewing my growth as a rejection of them or the life we had shared. This wasn't always easy to navigate. I had to learn to accept that not everyone would understand or support my journey, and that was okay. My transformation wasn't about pleasing others; it was about becoming the person I was meant to be.

One of the most unexpected lessons I learned was that change, though deeply personal, is rarely solitary. Even when it felt isolating, my growth had an impact on the people and spaces around me. My commitment to healing set a new standard for the relationships I allowed into my life. It pushed me to seek out connections built on mutual respect, empathy, and authenticity. It also forced me to reevaluate relationships that no longer aligned with my values or my vision for the future. Letting go of those relationships was painful, but it was necessary to make room for the new.

The emotional weight of change also brought a new kind of clarity. It taught me that healing isn't about returning to who you were before the pain; it's about becoming someone stronger, wiser, and more compassionate because of it. I began to see my past not as a series of unfortunate events, but as a series of lessons, each one teaching me something valuable about myself and the world. This shift in perspective allowed me to approach life with greater gratitude and hope, even in the face of challenges.

Change also taught me patience—with myself, with others, and with the process. I learned that healing doesn't happen on a schedule. It takes time to unravel years of pain, to rebuild trust in yourself and in others, and to create a life that reflects your true values and desires. I had to give myself grace, to celebrate small victories and forgive myself for setbacks. Each step, no matter how small, was a win that celebrated my strength and determination.

Looking back, I see that the decision to change was about creating a new narrative for my life. It was about choosing to believe in my worth, even when others didn't. It was about daring to dream of a life where I wasn't just surviving, but thriving. And it was about understanding that change, no matter how heavy it feels, is always worth the effort when it leads you closer to becoming the person you were always meant to be.

A NEW BEGINNING

The heart is where transformation truly begins. It is not in the external circumstances or the resolutions we make to change what's outside of us. It starts deep within—in the quiet, raw moments of self-reflection when you dare to confront the truths you've been running from. These are the moments when you ask yourself the hard questions: Who am I, beyond the roles I play? What do I believe about my worth? What does it mean to truly live a life that reflects the desires of my heart?

For me, this transformation began when I made a decision: to love myself the way God loves me—unconditionally and without reservation. That decision wasn't a single act, but a journey, an unfolding process that required me to dismantle the narratives I had carried for so long. For years, I believed that love had to be earned, that worthiness was something I had to prove through perfection, sacrifice, or achievement. But God's love showed me otherwise. His love wasn't conditional on my performance; it existed simply because I did. Learning to embrace that truth was both liberating and transformative.

Breaking free from the generational cycles that had kept my family bound was one of the hardest, but most necessary parts of this journey. These cycles—rooted in pain, trauma, and patterns of survival—had shaped not only my parents, but their parents before them. They were woven into the fabric of my upbringing, influencing how I viewed myself, my relationships, and the world around me. It would have been easy to let those patterns continue, to resign myself to a life defined by what I had inherited. But I knew that wasn't the life I wanted for myself, nor the legacy I wanted to live or leave behind.

Breaking those cycles required more than just intention—it required action. I had to confront the beliefs that had taken root in my heart, beliefs that told me I was unworthy, that love was fleeting, and that happiness was always just out of reach. I had to unlearn behaviors born out of fear and survival, replacing them with ones rooted in trust and hope. And perhaps most importantly, I had to forgive—not just others, but myself. Forgiveness became the bridge between the life I had lived and the life I wanted to create.

In many ways, this chapter of my life was about waking up to the truth of who I was and who I was created to be. It was about realizing that the journey to becoming whole doesn't begin with fixing the world around you—it begins within, in the places of the heart that are often hidden even from yourself. It begins with the courage to look inward, to sit with your pain, and to believe that something beautiful can come from it.

This awakening was also a declaration of worthiness. For so long, I had believed that my value was tied to what I could give to others, to how well I could meet their expectations or how much I could endure without breaking. But I began to understand that worthiness isn't something you earn; it's something you claim. I started to believe that I was worthy of love, joy, and a life that reflected the deepest desires of my heart—not because of anything I had done, but simply because I was created with intention and purpose.

The path to transformation is rarely linear, and mine was no exception. There were moments of doubt, moments when the weight of change felt too heavy to carry. But each step forward, no matter how small, was a testament to my resilience, perseverance, and my belief in the possibility of a better future. I began to see the pieces of my past not as burdens, but as building blocks for something greater. The wounds I had carried became reminders of my strength, and the lessons I had learned became tools for growth.

As I embraced this new beginning, I realized that transformation is not about erasing the past. It's about integrating it—honoring the experiences that have shaped you while refusing to let them define you. It's about finding meaning in the pain, discovering purpose in the struggles, and using those lessons as fuel to move forward.

In the hidden places of my heart, transformation began. It was the first step on a path that would lead me toward a life of meaning, strength, and unwavering hope. And as I continue on this journey, I carry with me the lessons of my past, not as burdens, but as reminders of how far I've come and how much further I can go. This is the promise of a new beginning: that no matter where you start, you can always choose to rewrite your story. And this, for me, was just the beginning.

SELF-AWARENESS AND REFLECTION

1. Acknowledging Deferred Hope: Reflect on a time when you felt like your dreams or desires were delayed or unfulfilled. How did it affect your emotions, self-perception, or relationships?

_____

_____

_____

_____

_____

_____

_____

_____

_____

2. Generational Influence: What patterns or beliefs have been passed down in your family that you may have unconsciously inher-ited? Are there any you feel ready to address or change?

_____

_____

_____

_____

_____

_____

_____

_____

_____

_____

_____

3. Forgiveness Journey: Who or what do you need to forgive—not to excuse their actions, but to release the hold of pain on your heart?

_____

_____

_____

_____

_____

_____

_____

_____

_____

_____

_____

_____

_____

4. Faith and Healing: How has your faith or belief system helped you navigate difficult times? What role does it play in your personal growth?

_____

_____

_____

_____

_____

_____

_____

_____

_____

_____

_____

_____

5. Emotional Awakening: Identify an emotion you've been avoiding or suppressing. What might happen if you gave yourself permission to fully feel it?

_____

_____

_____

_____

_____

_____

_____

_____

_____

_____

_____

_____

TIPS FOR HEALING MATTERS OF THE HEART

- *Name Your Pain:* Healing starts with identifying and naming the emotions and experiences that have shaped your heart. Avoidance only deepens the wound.

- *Create Emotional Boundaries:* Protect your emotional well-being by setting boundaries with those who may trigger or perpetuate old wounds.

- *Practice Gratitude:* Even amidst pain, gratitude for small joys and victories can be a powerful tool for shifting your perspective.

- *Seek Support:* Surround yourself with people who listen, encourage, and support you in your journey of healing.

- *Prioritize Self-Love:* Learn to love and accept yourself as you are, imperfections and all. The relationship you have with yourself sets the tone for all others.

How can you implement the aforementioned tips in your daily life?

_____
_____
_____
_____
_____
_____
_____
_____
_____
_____
_____
_____
_____
_____
_____

QUOTES TO INSPIRE

"Hope deferred makes the heart sick, but a longing fulfilled is a tree of life." Proverbs 13:12

"Forgiveness is not an occasional act; it is a constant attitude." – Martin Luther King Jr.

"Healing doesn't mean the damage never existed. It means the damage no longer controls your life." – Unknown

After reflecting on these quotes, journal your thoughts below.

_____

_____

_____

_____

_____

_____

_____

_____

_____

_____

_____

_____

_____

_____

_____

_____

_____

_____

_____

_____

_____

_____

_____

_____

_____

_____

_____

_____

_____

CHAPTER THREE

A Better Me, A Better You

L ife has a way of pushing us into roles we never imagined for ourselves, forcing us to rise or crumble under the weight of unexpected responsibilities. For me, that moment came with motherhood. Becoming a mother was both a defining challenge and the greatest blessing of my life. It shifted my perspective, transforming how I viewed myself, my purpose, and the world around me. It was no longer just about surviving; it was about growing, thriving, and creating a better future—not just for myself, but for my daughter.

Motherhood taught me that self-improvement isn't solely for myself—it's a gift to the people we love. The better I became, the more I could pour into my daughter and others around me. This chapter of my life wasn't just about navigating life's challenges. It was about rising to meet them with courage and grace. It was about embracing the transformation that motherhood demanded of me and finding beauty in the process. It taught me that within the weight of responsibility lies the opportunity for extraordinary growth. And in that growth, I found not only my strength, but also a deep sense of purpose that would carry me through the challenges yet to come.

THE TRANSITION TO MOTHERHOOD

Motherhood wasn't part of my immediate plans, but when it came into my life, it brought a whirlwind of emotions—fear, uncertainty, love, and an unshakable sense of responsibility. I never envisioned becoming a single mother or perpetuating the cycle of fatherlessness I had grown up with, but life has a way of redirecting our paths. When my relationship with my daughter's father fell apart, it marked the end of one chapter, but the beginning of a journey I knew I would have to walk alone. His absence left a void—a devastating realization that I wouldn't have the partnership I'd once imagined. But in that void, something powerful emerged: a fire, a fierce deter-mination to give my daughter everything I had missed, even if it meant facing the world alone.

The early days of motherhood were some of the most challenging yet transformative moments of my life. Sleepless nights blurred into exhausting days as I navigated the endless demands of caring for a newborn. Every cry, every sleepless night, every worry weighed on me, but it also strengthened my resolve. I quickly learned that moth-erhood was as much about sacrifice as it was about love. I had to make decisions that forced me to let go of parts of myself—relation-ships that didn't serve us, dreams that no longer aligned with my reality, and even the comfort of putting my needs first.

Those sacrifices weren't easy, but they were necessary. Each one was rooted in a single, unwavering belief: my daughter deserved a life of stability, love, and opportunity. I was determined to be more than I'd ever been for her, to ensure she had the foundation I had often longed for. She became my greatest motivation. Every choice I made, no matter how small, was driven by the thought of her future.

There were moments when the weight of responsibility felt unbearable. I often questioned whether I was strong enough, resourceful enough, or capable enough to give her what she deserved. But in moments of doubt, I found strength in her presence. Her tiny hand gripping mine reminded me that she wasn't just depending on me, she believed in me, even when I struggled to believe in myself.

The transition to motherhood was a shift from survival to growth, from living for myself to living for someone far greater. Every challenge became an opportunity to prove to myself—and to her—that I could rise, adapt, and overcome. In many ways, motherhood didn't just transform my life; it saved it. It gave me purpose, resilience, and a reason to keep moving forward, even when the odds felt stacked against me.

She wasn't merely my child; she was my reason, my "why," the force that turned fear into courage and uncertainty into determination. Together, we were building a new foundation, one rooted in love, sacrifice, and the belief that no matter where we started, we could create something better.

PERSONAL RESPONSIBILITY AND SACRIFICES

Motherhood has a way of sharpening your focus, forcing you to confront your own shortcomings and take full responsibility for the life you want to build—not just for yourself, but for the little one depending on you. For me, becoming a mother meant no longer living reactively. It required an intentionality I hadn't fully embraced before, a shift in mindset that demanded I plan, sacrifice, and strive for something better. My daughter deserved a future filled with possibility, and it was up to me to create that foundation.

When my daughter was just a few months old, I found myself living in a low-income housing unit, relying on public assistance, and juggling multiple jobs to keep the lights on and food on the table. It wasn't the life I had envisioned, but it was the reality I faced —and I faced it with grit and determination. I refused to let our circumstances define us. To me, those challenges weren't a stopping point; they were proving ground. Every late-night shift, every meal stretched to last a little longer, every tear shed in exhaustion-- it all represented my commitment to giving my daughter a better life.

But the weight of responsibility didn't come without its struggles. I often felt the sting of rejection, a pain that cut deeper than I expected. My daughter's father chose to distance himself, a decision that left a gaping hole not just in my life, but in hers. That rejection wasn't just personal—it felt generational, a painful echo of the fatherlessness I had known in my own childhood. On top of that, relationships with family members, especially my mother, grew increasingly strained. Instead of being my safety net, I often felt like I was navigating life alone, with no one to lean on during my hardest moments.

Yet, even in those dark times, I chose to focus on what I could control. I couldn't change the decisions of others, but I could control my own response to them. I could choose to rise above, to work harder, and to show my daughter what resilience looked like. I refused to let rejection or strained relationships derail my vision of the future. Instead, I used those moments as fuel to push forward.

The sacrifices I made along the way were countless, but they came with valuable lessons. I learned to stretch every dollar, to live frugally, and to plan. My dreams didn't die under the weight of my circumstances; they adapted. I no longer viewed success as something grand or distant, but found it in the small victories—the first stable home I provided for my daughter, the joy of hearing her laughter despite our struggles, the pride of overcoming obstacles that once seemed insurmountable.

Through it all, motherhood taught me the power of leading by example. If I wanted my daughter to grow up strong, confident, and full of hope, I knew I had to embody those qualities myself. I couldn't just tell her to dream big; I had to show her what it looked like to work tirelessly toward a dream, to face challenges with grace and determination. Every sacrifice I made, every moment of doubt I pushed through, became a living example of resilience for her to follow.

And while the road was anything, but easy, I came to understand that these sacrifices were not just for her—they were for me, too.

They were the building blocks of a better version of myself, one who could rise above adversity and turn pain into purpose. In my daughter, I found the ultimate reason to strive for more. She didn't just depend on me for survival; she inspired me to grow, to thrive, and to never settle for less than the best we could achieve.

MOMENTS OF RESILIENCE

Life often tests us in ways we least expect, pushing us to the brink and forcing us to choose between surrender and resilience. For me, the curveballs came fast and hard, leaving me breathless, but never broken. From losing my home to navigating health scares, the challenges seemed unrelenting. Yet, in the face of every setback, I made a choice: I would not let my circumstances define me. I would rise—not just for myself, but for my daughter and the vision I held for our future.

One of the most trying times was when I found myself homeless, living out of my car with nowhere to turn. Yet, by God's grace, I didn't look like what I was going through. The weight of uncertainty was suffocating, but I refused to let it crush me. Every morning, I woke up determined to keep moving forward, no matter how challenging the road ahead seemed. I leaned on the kindness of others, finding temporary shelter with generous individuals who offered us a lifeline when I needed it most. Their belief in me served as a reminder that even in the darkest of times, there is light—there are people who care, who see your worth, and who extend a hand when the world feels like it's falling apart.

During this time, I was faced with a crossroads that would shape the rest of my life. I could have allowed despair to consume me, but instead, I chose to fight. I enrolled in classes, pursued certifications, and refused to let my dreams slip away. Some days, I would attend school and then return to a borrowed space to sleep, all while juggling the responsibilities of motherhood. My car became a makeshift storage unit, my determination-- my only constant. With every small victory, I built a foundation—not just for stability, but for growth.

The challenges I faced taught me lessons I couldn't have learned any other way. I discovered the value of humility, realizing that asking for help isn't a weakness, but a sign of your strength. It takes courage to admit that you can't do it all on your own. Leaning on the kindness and support of others wasn't easy, but it was necessary. It reminded me of the power of community and the importance of giving back when you can, because no one succeeds entirely on their own.

These moments also revealed a reservoir of resilience within me that I didn't know existed. Each challenge, each obstacle, became an opportunity to prove to myself that I was capable of more than I had ever imagined. Every time I pushed through the pain, uncertainty, or exhaustion, I felt a piece of the weight of survival begin to lift, replaced by a growing sense of purpose and strength. I wasn't just surviving anymore—I was building a life, brick by brick, moment by moment.

Those experiences shaped me into the person I am today. They taught me that resilience isn't just about enduring hardship; it's about finding the courage to rebuild, even when the odds are stacked against you. They reminded me that life's toughest moments often hold the seeds of transformation. And perhaps most importantly, they reaffirmed my belief that I wasn't alone—there was a network of people, seen and unseen, cheering me on and helping me to rise.

In those moments of resilience, I discovered that adversity wasn't my enemy—it was my teacher. It showed me how to keep going when the road ahead seemed endless, how to find strength in vulnerability, and how to transform survival into thriving. It was through these trials that I found not only my footing, but also the confidence to pursue a future I could be proud of, for both myself and my daughter.

SHIFTING FROM SURVIVAL TO GROWTH

Motherhood became the lens through which I redefined my life's purpose. It was no longer enough to survive day by day; I wanted to create a life filled with opportunity, hope, and abundance—for both myself and my daughter. Her presence was a call to action, a reminder that I couldn't allow my struggles to dictate the narrative of her life. I wanted her to see, through my actions, that challenges are not dead ends—they are invitations to grow.

This transition from survival to growth wasn't an easy, smooth process. It required a complete rewiring of my mindset. I had to confront the limiting beliefs that had kept me tethered to survival mode for so long—the fear of failure, the desire for external valida-tion, and the doubts about my own worthiness. These weren't easy chains to break. They had been forged over years of hardship and reinforced by the societal and generational pressures I carried. But for my daughter's sake, I had to dismantle them, one by one.

Faith became my compass in this transformative journey. There were days when the road ahead was obscured, when fear threatened to pull me back into old habits. In those moments, I leaned into my faith. I prayed for guidance, for strength, for the courage to keep moving forward even when the destination seemed impossibly far away. God's word reminded me that I wasn't walking this path alone, that He had a plan for my life and that of my daughter's—a plan that required me to trust, to let go of fear, and to embrace the possibility of something greater.

Letting go of the need for external validation was one of the most liberating aspects of this shift. For so long, I had looked to others for approval, for reassurance that I was on the right path. But mother-hood taught me that my worth didn't come from the opinions of others—it came from God. My daughter didn't need a perfect mother; she needed a present one, a resilient one, a mother who could show her what it meant to rise after every fall.

The changes I made began to bear fruit in both of our lives. My daughter thrived, not because of the material things I worked to provide, but because of the love, stability, and hope that filled our home. I could see her joy and confidence growing, and it reaffirmed everything I was working toward. She was living proof that my efforts were not in vain, that every sacrifice, every moment of self-doubt, and every hard-won victory was building a foundation for a brighter future.

This shift also changed the way I saw myself. I began to embrace growth as a lifelong journey, not a destination. I learned to celebrate progress, no matter how small, and to see setbacks as opportunities to learn and improve. The same lessons I wanted to teach my daughter—that resilience can turn obstacles into stepping stones, that self-belief is a powerful tool—became the principles that guided my own life.

Shifting from survival to thriving required me shift from a fixed to a growth mindset. It was about choosing faith over fear, trusting that God's plan was greater than my circumstances, and believing in my ability to create a better future. For my daughter, and for myself, this journey highlighted the power of perseverance, love, and the unyielding belief that brighter days lie ahead. She was my inspiration, my "why" — and together we were building a life that was about thriving.

A BETTER ME, A BETTER YOU

The journey to becoming a better me was never just about my own self-improvement—it was about creating a ripple effect that would touch every aspect of my life and the lives of those around me. I came to realize that the work I did on myself wasn't confined to my personal growth. It spilled into the way I raised my daughter, the way I served my community, and the way I inspired those who crossed my path. Every breakthrough, every hard-earned lesson, became a gift not just for me, but for others.

Motherhood amplified this realization. My daughter helped me identify the values I wanted to instill in her and challenged me to embody them fully. I couldn't teach her resilience without demonstrating it. I couldn't expect her to believe in her worth if I didn't believe in mine. Every step I took toward becoming a better version of myself was a step toward giving her a brighter future. She was my motivation to rise above the circumstances that tried to hold me back, to push beyond the limits I once thought defined me.

But the impact didn't stop there. As I grew, I began to see how my journey could inspire and uplift others. I became more intentional in my interactions, more mindful of how my words and actions could plant seeds of hope in others. Whether it was a kind word to a struggling friend, mentorship to a young person, or simply leading by example, I understood that my transformation was part of a larger purpose. It wasn't just about me—it was about everyone whose lives I touched now and future generations.

Looking back, I can see how the challenges I faced became stepping stones toward something greater. Those moments of struggle and doubt were opportunities to grow stronger, wiser, and more compassionate. The same resilience that allowed me to rise above my circumstances became a source of strength for others. The lessons I learned—about perseverance, love, and the power of faith —are lessons I now share with those who are on their own journeys of transformation and holistic success.

Motherhood, I've learned, is about becoming the kind of person your child can look up to. It's about demonstrating what it means to overcome adversity with grace and determination, to lead with love, and to live with purpose. In striving to be a better mother, I became a better leader, a better friend, and a better servant of God's vision. The growth I experienced in one area of my life naturally extended to others, creating a cycle of positive change.

Faith played an essential role in this process. Through my relationship with God, I discovered that true strength lies in love, resilience, and the firm belief that we are capable of more than we imagine. This faith sustained me through my hardest days and gave me the courage to keep moving forward, even when the path was unclear. It reminded me that I wasn't walking this journey alone, that every step I took was guided by a purpose greater than myself.

I'm thankful for the challenges that shaped me, the people who supported me, and the unwavering love of God that carried me through. I've come to understand that the work of becoming a better me is ongoing, that each day brings new opportunities to grow, to serve, and to love more deeply. And in doing so, I hope to continue creating a better world—not just for myself, but for my daughter, my community, and the generations to come.

SELF-AWARENESS AND REFLECTION

1. Defining Your "Why": Reflect on what motivates you most in life. Who or what inspires you to keep going, even when the road is difficult?

_____

_____

_____

_____

_____

_____

_____

_____

_____

_____

2. Overcoming Challenges: Think about a time when life tested you. How did you rise to the occasion, and what did you learn about your resilience?

_____

_____

_____

_____

_____

_____

_____

_____

_____

_____

3. Personal Responsibility: What is one area of your life where you can take greater ownership? How can this change impact both you and those around you?

_____

_____

_____

_____

_____

_____

_____

_____

_____

_____

4. Sacrifice and Growth: Identify a sacrifice you've made for a greater purpose. How has it shaped your character or opened doors to new opportunities?

_____

_____

_____

_____

_____

_____

_____

_____

_____

_____

5. Shifting Mindsets: Are there areas of your life where you are still operating in "survival mode"? What steps can you take to shift toward a mindset of growth and thriving?

_____

_____

_____

_____

_____

_____

_____

_____

_____

_____

_____

_____

TIPS FOR NAVIGATING LIFE'S CHALLENGES

- *Embrace Small Wins:* Celebrate the progress you make, no matter how small. Every step forward is a step closer to your goals.

- *Be Adaptable:* Life may not go as planned, but flexibility and openness to change can lead to unexpected opportunities.

- *Create a Support System:* Lean on people who uplift and encourage you. Community, mentorship, and counseling are invaluable during challenging times.

- *Focus on Your Sphere of Control:* Concentrate on what you can change and let go of the things outside your control.

- *Lead by Example:* Remember that your actions influence others, especially those who look up to you. Be the person you want others to emulate.

How can you implement the aforementioned tips in your daily life?

_____

_____

_____

_____

_____

_____

_____

_____

_____

_____

_____

_____

_____

QUOTES TO INSPIRE

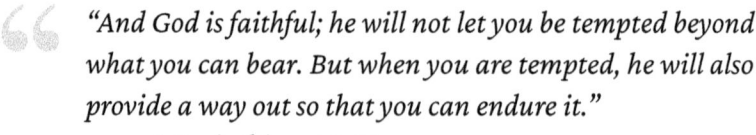

"And God is faithful; he will not let you be tempted beyond what you can bear. But when you are tempted, he will also provide a way out so that you can endure it."
– 1 Corinthians 10:13

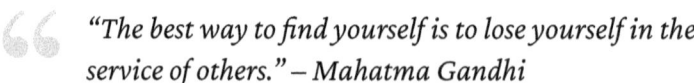

"The best way to find yourself is to lose yourself in the service of others." – Mahatma Gandhi

"Resilience is knowing that you are the only one that has the power and the responsibility to pick yourself up."
– Mary Holloway

After reflecting on these quotes, journal your thoughts below.

_____
_____
_____
_____
_____
_____
_____
_____
_____
_____
_____
_____
_____
_____
_____
_____
_____
_____
_____
_____
_____
_____
_____
_____
_____
_____
_____
_____
_____

CHAPTER FOUR

Finding Your Voice

T he journey to finding your voice is often messy— marked by moments of silence, fear, and doubt. It began with a simple decision to pursue higher education—a decision that would not only alter the course of my life, but would also become the foundation of my purpose. Getting my degree was about discovering who I was, what I stood for, and the potency of my voice.

THE JOURNEY TO COLLEGE

Arriving in DeKalb, Illinois, felt like stepping into the unknown. I hadn't planned to move there—it was a decision born out of necessity, not ambition. Life had left me no other choice. Homeless and desperate for a sense of stability, I accepted an offer for low-income housing, hoping to build a foundation for myself and my daughter. I thought this would be a fresh start, a chance to catch my breath and regain control of my life. At the time, my goal was simple: to complete a certification program and secure a steady job that would allow us to survive.

But life had other plans.

Sitting in the advisor's office at the local community college, I felt a mix of apprehension and determination. I explained my plan to earn a certificate, confident that this would be a quick and practical way to enter the workforce. Then came the question that would change everything: *"What do you want to do?"*

I hesitated, caught off guard. The truth was, I hadn't thought much about what I truly wanted. My focus had always been on survival, not dreams or aspirations. Social work had lingered in the back of my mind—a natural extension of the work I'd done in the community and the passion I felt for helping others. I shared this with the advisor, thinking it was a safe and achievable answer.

Her response was direct: *"You need a bachelor's degree for that."* Her words landed heavily. A bachelor's degree? That felt like a luxury, an unattainable goal for someone like me. I had bills to pay, a daughter to raise, and no time to indulge in the fantasy of higher education. The thought of spending years in school while struggling to make ends meet seemed overwhelming.

Still, the advisor persisted. She didn't let me walk away from the possibility of something greater. She spoke with conviction, outlining the steps I could take and assuring me that it was possible, even if it didn't feel like it at that moment. Despite my reservations, her confidence sparked something in me—a small flicker of hope.

Reluctantly, I agreed to pursue my Associate's degree, but not without laying down my terms. "I'll do it," I told her, "but only if I'm close to graduating can I consider a Bachelor's program." It was a reluctant promise, a compromise between my pragmatic fears and the faintest belief that maybe, just maybe, there was more waiting for me.

At the time, the commitment felt insurmountable. I was a single mother balancing the demands of work, childcare, and survival. Yet, looking back, that conversation marked a pivotal moment in my journey—a moment when I chose to bet on myself, even in the face of uncertainty.

What I didn't realize then was that this decision would become the catalyst for transformation. It was more than simply earning a degree. This journey was about discovering my potential, finding my voice, and rewriting the narrative of my life. In that small advisor's office, a seed was planted—a seed that would grow into something far greater than I could have imagined.

DISCOVERING MY IDENTITY

As I progressed through college, I realized that the journey was for me— discovering "me" at my core. The academic environment, though intimidating at first, became a crucible for personal growth, challenging me to confront my insecurities and redefine my sense of self. I learned that I was a non-traditional student, balancing motherhood, work, and school, and a first-generation college student— navigating a world that was entirely foreign to me. Every step felt like uncharted territory, and I often questioned if I truly belonged.

From the moment I walked into my first classroom, it was clear that college would push me beyond my comfort zone. Writing papers, participating in discussions, and grappling with academic concepts felt like an uphill battle. Imposter syndrome loomed large, whispering that I wasn't smart enough, prepared enough, or worthy enough to be in these spaces. Yet, with each challenge, I began to uncover a resilience I hadn't realized I possessed. College was a place of learning that reflected back the strength and determination I carried all along.

Each assignment and lecture acted as a stepping stone toward self-awareness. I began to see my experiences, not as isolated struggles, but as pieces of a larger narrative. I learned to articulate my journey, to name the challenges I had faced, and to analyze the systemic barriers that shaped my life. The language of academia became a tool for intellectual growth and personal empowerment. It allowed me to contextualize my life experiences and see my challenges not as failures, but as opportunities for transformation.

One of the most profound moments of self-discovery came through a mentor who introduced me to Maslow's hierarchy of needs. She explained how unmet basic needs—safety, security, belonging—could hinder personal and professional growth. The concept resonated deeply. I realized that many of the struggles I had faced weren't due to a lack of capability, but to the weight of unmet needs that had shaped my reality. Armed with this new framework, I began advocating for myself in ways I never had before.

In meetings, when I felt unseen or unheard, I would confidently state, "My Maslow's hierarchy of needs is not being met." It was a simple yet powerful statement that forced others to pause and consider the human side of the decisions they were making. For the first time, I felt heard. This tool became a cornerstone of my advocacy—not just for myself, but for others who, like me, felt voiceless in systems that often overlooked their humanity.

The experience of speaking up, of asserting my needs and values, was transformative. I found my voice and reclaimed my identity. I began to see myself as more than a student or a mother; I saw myself as a leader, a change-maker, and a force for good. College gave me the language to describe my struggles and the courage to face them head-on, and in doing so, it helped me uncover the best version of myself.

THE POWER OF COMMUNITY & MENTORSHIP

Throughout my college journey, I was blessed to find mentors who became my anchors during turbulent times. They weren't just advisors or professors going through the motions; they were lifelines—people who saw potential in me when I struggled to see it in myself. Their belief in me became a source of strength, pushing me to rise above self-doubt and the weight of my circumstances.

One such mentor was a representative from Northern Illinois University. When I presented her with a meticulously mapped-out academic plan during a recruitment event, she was so impressed that she offered me a job in Admissions on the spot. That opportunity was an affirmation of my capability and worth. It was the first time I felt recognized for my potential rather than defined by my struggles. That moment became a turning point, showing me that my voice, my story, and my efforts mattered.

At Northern Illinois University, I found a community that became a foundation for my personal and academic growth. Spaces like the *Center for Black Studies* and the *TRIO Program* became my safe-havens. These programs provided not only resources, but also a sense of belonging that I hadn't realized I was missing. In these spaces, I met people who understood my struggles—many of them had walked similar paths—and they celebrated my victories, no matter how small.

The *TRIO Program*, designed to support first-generation and low-income students, became a transformative part of my journey. Through *TRIO*, I found opportunities to explore new horizons, including my first trips outside of Illinois. Traveling to New York and Florida for conferences and service-learning projects broadened my perspective and showed me that the world was bigger than I had ever imagined. These experiences helped me see beyond my immediate challenges and inspired me to dream bigger for myself and my daughter.

The Center for Black Studies became a refuge where I could connect with mentors who shared my cultural experiences and understood the unique challenges I faced as a Black woman navigating a predominantly white institution. One mentor in particular taught me how to articulate my needs by using language that demanded attention and respect. When I expressed my frustrations about being overlooked, she introduced me to the concept of Maslow's hierarchy of needs and encouraged me to use it as a tool for self-advocacy. With her guidance, I found the confidence to stand up for myself and to assert, "My Maslow's hierarchy of needs is not being met." That simple, yet impactful statement became a personal slogan that forced others to consider my humanity and present barriers.

These mentors and the communities they fostered helped me academically; it has also helped me grow as a person. They taught me the power of resilience, the importance of self-advocacy, and the value of leaning on others for support. They reminded me that I didn't have to navigate this journey alone. For the first time, I felt like I belonged in a space where my voice and my experiences were valued.

The connections I made at Northern Illinois University weren't limited to faculty and staff; they extended to fellow students who became my allies and friends. Together, we navigated the challenges of balancing coursework, jobs, and personal responsibilities. We celebrated each other's successes and supported one another through setbacks. This network of support became a vital part of my journey, reinforcing that I was never truly alone.

Through the mentorship and community, I began to see myself not just as a student, but as a leader. I learned that my struggles had given me a unique perspective and that my voice could be a powerful tool for change. These experiences shaped my understanding of the importance of uplifting others and taught me that when we invest in each other, we all rise together.

OVERCOMING CHALLENGES

The path to higher education was fraught with obstacles, many of which felt insurmountable at times. As a single mother, I carried the weight of multiple responsibilities—juggling parenting, academics, and several jobs with little margin for error. Every day was a balancing act, where the stakes felt impossibly high. Missing a class or shift at work could set me back days, even weeks. Yet, I pressed orward, fueled by the desire to create a better future for my daughter and myself.

However, the challenges weren't just logistical—they were

deeply systemic. As a Black woman navigating predominantly white academic spaces, I often felt the sting of racism, bias, and microgression. Professors dismissed my lived experiences as anecdotal, insisting that only published research carried legitimacy. I vividly recall moments when I spoke up in class, only to be met with skepticism or outright dismissal. My insights, born from firsthand experience, were undervalued because they didn't fit neatly into the frameworks of academic theory.

The pressure to conform was constant. I felt the unspoken demand to "code-switch"—to alter my speech, demeanor, and even the way I presented myself to fit the expectations of these spaces. It was exhausting and alienating because I refused to lose myself to fit the status quo. There were days when I questioned whether I truly belonged, whether the sacrifices I was making were worth it, and whether I had the strength to continue.

But through these struggles, I began to uncover a deeper truth: my lived experience was not a liability—it was a strength. I realized that my perspective, shaped by my journey through poverty, systemic inequities, and resilience, gave me a voice that was both unique and necessary. It allowed me to bridge the gap between academic theory and real-world application, to speak authentically about the issues that academic research often sanitized or ignored. My story carried weight, and I refused to let anyone diminish its value.

Finding my voice wasn't easy. It required me to confront the internalized doubts that had taken root from years of systemic oppression. I had to believe that my experiences were valid, that they deserved to be shared, and that they could make a difference. Slowly, I began to use my voice as a tool—not just for myself, but for others who felt silenced in similar ways. I spoke up in classrooms, challenged biases, and shared my perspective with conviction. Each time I did, I felt a little more grounded in my identity and purpose.

Through these experiences, I learned to navigate the tension between adapting to academic norms and staying true to myself. I found ways to integrate my lived experiences into my work, creating a narrative that was both scholarly and authentic. Instead of allowing the system to silence me, I began to carve out a space where I could thrive on my terms.

These challenges ultimately strengthened my resolve. They taught me that resilience is about refusing to let those hardships define you. It's about taking the pain, the doubt, and the barriers— transforming them into stepping stones for growth. I realized that I didn't need to change who I was to fit into these spaces. Instead, I needed to change how these spaces viewed voices like mine. And I did. One step, one class, one voice at a time.

FINDING PURPOSE THROUGH FAITH

Through every high and low, my relationship with God was the unshakable foundation that held me steady. Faith was the compass that guided my decisions and the source of strength that carried me through moments of doubt and despair. When the world seemed overwhelming and the obstacles felt too heavy to bear, my faith reminded me that I was never truly alone. God was with me every step of the way, orchestrating a plan far greater than I could see in the moment.

One of the most profound lessons I learned during this time was that God doesn't simply equip us for survival—He equips us for purpose. Every trial, every setback, every heartache was not wasted. These experiences were refining me, preparing me for the work I was called to do. Faith gave me the courage to look beyond my immediate struggles and trust in the bigger picture, even when that picture was unclear.

There were countless moments when I felt like giving up, but God always showed up, often in unexpected ways. He placed people in my life at the exact moments I needed them—mentors who believed in me, friends who encouraged me, and strangers whose kindness reminded me of His grace. These divine connections were reminders that God was orchestrating every detail of my journey.

Faith also redefined how I saw my challenges. What once felt like insurmountable obstacles began to look like opportunities for growth. My struggles strengthened my character and deepened my trust in God's plan. I began to understand that the pain I endured wasn't meaningless—it was shaping me into the person I needed to become to fulfill my purpose.

Walking in faith required me to surrender the need for control and embrace a trust that was sometimes uncomfortable. It meant believing in the unseen, in promises that had yet to be fulfilled, and in the knowledge that God was working all things together for my good. It wasn't always easy. There were moments of frustration, of questioning, of wondering why the path had to be so difficult. But each time I brought those questions to God, He met me with reassurance and guidance.

One of the most transformative realizations was that God's plans for me were not limited to what I could imagine for myself. He didn't just want me to survive—He wanted me to thrive, to walk boldly in the purpose He had designed for me. Every class I took, every challenge I overcame, every moment of perseverance was part of a divine preparation process. My faith gave me the perspective to see that the journey itself was just as important as the destination.

Through faith, I found not just strength, but also clarity. I came to understand that my purpose wasn't just about personal success—it was about serving others, using my experiences and gifts to uplift and empower those around me. God had equipped me with a unique story and a unique voice, and He was calling me to use them for something greater than myself.

Faith became my anchor, my guide, and my greatest source of hope. It reminded me that even when the path was difficult, it was leading somewhere meaningful. With God's love as my foundation, I was able to navigate the challenges of life with courage and grace, knowing that every step was part of His plan for my life.

A VOICE FOR OTHERS

As I found my voice, I realized it wasn't just meant for me—it was meant to amplify the voices of others. Our voices are powerful tools for change, and I came to understand that true empowerment lies in using them to advocate, inspire, and uplift. It wasn't enough to simply speak for myself; I felt a calling to create spaces where others could feel heard, valued, and understood.

Finding my voice taught me the value of listening deeply. Advocacy begins not with speaking, but with understanding. I became attuned to the unspoken struggles of those around me—the student grappling with self-doubt, the single parent trying to juggle responsibilities, the community member feeling isolated and unheard. Their stories mirrored my own in many ways, and I knew from expe-rience how transformative it could be to have someone acknowledge your pain and your potential.

Through mentorship, I found one of the most impactful ways to give back. I sought to guide others, particularly those navigating the complexities of higher education or struggling to overcome systemic barriers. I shared my story to show others that they, too, were capable of overcoming obstacles. I wanted them to know they weren't alone—that someone believed in their worth and potential, even when they doubted it themselves.

Leadership became another avenue for using my voice to uplift others. Whether it was through community initiatives, organizing resources, or advocating for equitable policies, I discovered the power of collective action. I recognized that leadership wasn't about wielding authority, but about empowering those around me to see their own strength and agency. By standing up for what was right, I hoped to inspire others to do the same, as they developed their identity.

Advocacy became a central part of my purpose. I worked to challenge injustices, to question the systems that perpetuated inequality, and to push for changes that would make life better for those coming after me. I became a bridge—connecting people to opportunities, resources, and support that could transform their circumstances. Whether it was a struggling student seeking guidance, a colleague in need of encouragement, or a community member looking for a helping hand, I wanted to be a source of hope and a reminder that no one has to journey alone.

My own experiences taught me that the act of being heard can be life-changing. It validates our struggles, honors our efforts, and reminds us of our inherent worth. I wanted to create those moments for others, to be the person who listened when they felt unseen and who encouraged them when they felt unsure. The voice I had fought so hard to find became my greatest tool for ensuring that others could find theirs.

In giving others the space to speak and the confidence to use their voices, I found deeper meaning in my own journey. Every story shared, every barrier broken, was a testament to the power of connection and the resilience of the human spirit. Together, our voices became a symphony of strength and hope, capable of creating change in ways I had never imagined.

Speaking up is not always easy—it requires courage, vulnerability, and a willingness to confront both internal and external barriers. But it is through this process that we discover the depths of our strength and the boundlessness of our potential.

The power of voice lies in its ability to heal—not only ourselves, but those who hear us. When we share our stories, we give others permission to embrace their own. When we advocate for what is right, we pave the way for collective progress. And when we stand firm in who we are, we remind others of their own ability to do the same.

SELF-AWARENESS AND REFLECTION

1. Exploring Your Voice: Reflect on a time when you felt silenced. What prevented you from speaking up, and how can you reclaim that space now?

_____
_____
_____
_____
_____
_____
_____
_____
_____
_____

2. Strength in Struggle: Think about a challenging experience that shaped you. How has it contributed to your identity or given you a unique perspective?

_____
_____
_____
_____
_____
_____
_____
_____
_____
_____
_____

3. Your Purpose: What is something you feel deeply passionate about? How can you use your voice to advocate for that cause or issue?

_____

_____

_____

_____

_____

_____

_____

_____

_____

_____

_____

_____

_____

4. Mentors and Influences: Who has inspired or supported you on your journey? How have they helped you find or amplify your voice?

_____

_____

_____

_____

_____

_____

_____

_____

_____

_____

_____

_____

_____

5. *Listening to Others:* Consider someone whose voice is often over-looked. What can you do to create space for them to be heard?

_____

_____

_____

_____

_____

_____

_____

_____

_____

_____

_____

_____

TIPS FOR FINDING YOUR VOICE

- *Start Small:* Speak up in situations where you feel safe, gradually building confidence to use your voice in larger contexts.

- *Know Your Worth:* Remind yourself that your experiences and perspectives are valid and worthy of being shared.

- *Find Your Community:* Surround yourself with people who value your voice and encourage you to express yourself authentically.

- *Seek Mentorship:* Seek out mentors who can guide and inspire you, providing valuable insights on navigating spaces where your voice matters and helping you build the confidence to self-advocate effectively.

- *Embrace Vulnerability*: Recognize that using your voice may feel uncomfortable at times, but it's in those moments of vulnerability that your power shines.

How can you implement the aforementioned tips in your daily life?

_____

_____

_____

_____

_____

_____

_____

_____

_____

_____

_____

_____

_____

_____

_____

_____

QUOTES TO INSPIRE

"Faith comes by hearing, and hearing by the word of God."
— *Romans 10:17*

"There is no greater agony than bearing an untold story inside you." – Maya Angelou

"Speak up, even if your voice shakes." – Maggie Kuhn

71

After reflecting on these quotes, journal your thoughts below.

_____
_____
_____
_____
_____
_____
_____
_____
_____
_____
_____
_____
_____
_____
_____
_____
_____
_____
_____
_____
_____
_____
_____
_____
_____
_____
_____
_____
_____

CHAPTER FIVE

Breaking Generational Curses

Generational curses are deeply ingrained cycles of poverty, trauma, and limiting beliefs passed down through families. For me, these curses were all too real, manifesting as instability, unhealed wounds, conditional love, and a pervasive sense of unworthiness. The weight of these inherited patterns shaped my early life, but they also ignited a desire to break free—a determination to chart a new course for myself, my daughter, and for those who would follow.

DEFINING GENERATIONAL CURSES

In my family, generational curses were the invisible forces that bound us to cycles of pain, dysfunction, and limitation. They took the form of fractured relationships, economic struggles, and a perva-sive lack of emotional healing. These were patterns that repeated themselves across generations, passed down like heirlooms we never asked for.

My father carried the weight of his childhood, a life marked by neglect and abuse that shaped how he approached fatherhood and relationships. His pain, though unspoken, seeped into the fabric of our family, creating barriers where there should have been bridges. My mother, while fiercely strong in many ways, bore her own scars —unresolved traumas that spilled over into our home. Together, their unhealed wounds became the backdrop of my upbringing, teaching me lessons I would later have to unlearn.

These patterns shaped everything: how we communicated, how we loved, and how we coped with challenges. In my family, conflict was often met with silence or explosive outbursts, love was conditional, and self-worth was tied to approval from doing what people wanted. These unspoken rules governed how we interacted with one another and how we viewed the world around us. They became a lens through which I understood relationships, trust, and my place in the world.

At first, I didn't recognize these generational patterns for what they were. As a child, they felt normal because they were all I knew. But as I grew older and began to experience life outside of my family's sphere, I started to see how these dynamics limited us. I saw how unresolved pain could harden into bitterness, how unspoken trauma could manifest as anger, and how economic barriers could strip people of their dignity and dreams.

Recognizing these patterns was not an instant revelation, but a gradual process. It began with pain—the pain of repeating the same cycles in my own life. It took introspection to identify how much of my behavior, my choices, and even my fears were rooted in what I had absorbed growing up. I began to see these curses not as fate, but as chains—chains that could be broken with awareness, intention, and faith.

This realization ignited a desire within me for something better. I didn't want to perpetuate the same cycles of dysfunction to my daughter. I wanted to create a new legacy, one built on healing, love, perseverance, resilience. To do this, I had to face the uncomfortable truths and gain understanding about my family's history as well as my own tendencies. I had to confront the pain and make a conscious choice to live differently.

Breaking generational curses meant understanding where they came from and how they operated, but more importantly, it meant taking responsibility for my own healing. It wasn't about blaming my parents or my circumstances; it was about choosing to end the cycle and chart a new course. For me, this was a mission to ensure that my daughter would grow up free from the chains that had me bound. It was about rewriting the story, not just for myself, but for the generations to come.

MANIFESTATIONS OF CURSES

The generational curses that had shaped my family didn't disappear when I left home; they followed me, manifesting in ways that were both subtle and glaringly obvious. They showed up in my struggles—moments when fear seemed to paralyze me, when trust felt like a risk I couldn't afford, or when I doubted whether I was truly worthy of love. These weren't just fleeting thoughts or isolated moments; they were deeply ingrained patterns, a reflection of the emotional wounds I carried from my upbringing.

I saw these curses most vividly in my early relationships. The pain of rejection felt hauntingly familiar, as though it echoed the unspoken hurts of my childhood. I often found myself drawn to people who couldn't or wouldn't meet me where I was, perpetuating a cycle of unmet expectations and heartbreak. It wasn't until much later that I realized I was subconsciously reenacting the wounds of my past, seeking validation from people who were incapable of giving it.

The whispers of self-doubt were another painful reminder of these curses. They told me I wasn't good enough, that my dreams were too ambitious, too bold for someone like me. Whether it was pursuing education, taking a leap of faith in my career, or stepping into roles that required confidence, I constantly battled the voice inside that questioned my worth. It felt like an invisible weight, holding me back from fully embracing the opportunities that lay before me.

These curses weren't just external; they were internalized, influencing how I viewed myself and the decisions I made. I trusted the wrong people, often out of a desperate need to feel accepted, and I avoided opportunities out of fear of failure. I placed limitations on my own potential, not because I lacked capability, but because I couldn't yet see beyond the constraints of the past.

But perhaps the most profound and painful manifestation of these curses was the fear that I might pass them on to my daughter. The thought of her inheriting the same emotional wounds, the same fears and limitations that had held me back, was unbearable. I couldn't stand the idea of her growing up in the shadow of the same dysfunction that had shaped so much of my life.

This fear became both a burden and a catalyst. It filled me with dread, but it also fueled my determination to change. I resolved that her life would be different. She would grow up surrounded by love, stability, and the freedom to dream without limits. She would have the tools to face challenges with confidence, unencumbered by the chains that had bound me.

This resolution came at a cost. Breaking the cycle meant making sacrifices I could barely imagine, stepping into the unknown, and doing the hard work of confronting my own pain. It required unlearning the lessons of my past and replacing them with a new framework for love, trust, and resilience. But as overwhelming as it felt, I knew the alternative wasn't an option. My daughter deserved better, and so did I.

BREAKING THE PATTERNS

Breaking the chains of generational curses required far more than simply recognizing their existence—it required intentional, sustained action and a reliance on faith. It meant committing to a holistic process of transformation that would touch every corner of my life, from my choices and habits to the way I viewed relationships and defined success. This wasn't a journey I could undertake half-heartedly; it demanded a level of courage and humility I had never tapped into before.

The first and perhaps most difficult step was surrendering the need to protect myself. I had spent so much of my life fighting—fighting to survive, fighting to be heard, and fighting to overcome circumstances that seemed insurmountable. Letting go of that need to control and trust felt counterintuitive, even risky. But I began to realize that my survival instincts, though necessary in the past, were no longer serving me. I couldn't fix everything on my own, and I didn't have to. Surrendering was about giving it all over to God.

Surrender showed up in many forms. It appeared in moments of prayer, when I laid my burdens at God's feet and asked for His guidance. There were decisions I faced—about relationships, career, school, and parenting—that I didn't have the strength or clarity to make on my own. In those moments, I learned to trust God's plan, even when it didn't align with my expectations or when the path ahead was unclear. That trust was often accompanied by a quiet reassurance that I wasn't walking alone.

Forgiveness was another crucial element of breaking the patterns. Generational curses often stem from unresolved pain, and for me, that pain had hardened into anger and resentment toward those who had hurt me, knowingly or unknowingly. Carrying that resentment was like carrying a weight I couldn't afford to bear. Letting it go wasn't about excusing the harm done to me—it was about freeing myself from its hold.

Forgiveness came in layers. At first, it was about forgiving others: my parents for their shortcomings, people who had betrayed me, and even those who had perpetuated the very cycles I was trying to break. But perhaps the hardest forgiveness was directed inward. I had to confront the guilt and shame I carried for the mistakes I'd made, for the ways I had repeated harmful patterns before I understood them. It was only when I forgave myself that I could fully embrace the changes I was making.

Breaking the patterns also required vulnerability—a willingness to admit that I didn't have all the answers and that I needed help. This was especially difficult for someone like me, who had always prided herself on being strong and self-reliant. But I came to understand that vulnerability wasn't a weakness; it was a strength. It allowed me to lean on others despite prior disappointment, to accept support and wisdom from mentors, and to find solace in community. More importantly, it allowed me to open my heart to God's direction, trusting that He was working all things together for good, even when the process felt painful or slow.

There were sacrifices, too—decisions that forced me to choose between comfort and growth, between old habits and new possibilities. These sacrifices weren't easy, but they were necessary. They taught me discipline, perseverance, and the value of prioritizing long-term healing over short-term gratification. I learned to let go of relationships that were toxic, even when it hurt. I redefined success, focusing less on external validation and more on the inner work that would create a lasting lived legacy for my daughter and future generations.

Through it all, obedience became my compass. Obedience wasn't about blind compliance; it was about aligning my actions with my values, faith, and purpose. It was about listening for God's voice, even when it challenged me to step outside of my comfort zone, and responding with courage. Yielding to His plan meant accepting that I didn't always know what was best for me—but He did. And time and time again, I saw how obedience led to breakthroughs I couldn't have achieved on my own.

Breaking generational patterns wasn't a single act, but a series of deliberate choices, made again and again, even when the old ways tried to creep back in. It was a process of replacing fear with faith, bitterness with forgiveness, and control with surrender. It was about creating a new foundation, one built on love, resilience, and a commitment to healing. And as I walked this path, I realized that every step I took wasn't just for me—it was for my daughter, my family, and the generations yet to come. I became the cycle breaker and trailblazer.

STORIES OF TRANSFORMATION

One of the most profound breakthroughs in my journey came during a season of intense financial hardship. As a single mother, the weight of providing for my daughter often felt crushing, and there were times when I wrestled with feelings of inadequacy and loneliness. I vividly remember standing in my kitchen one evening, the cold light from the fridge illuminating its emptiness, while an overdue rent notice sat ominously on the counter. That moment was a culmination of so many fears—fears of failure and fears of repeating the struggles I had vowed to leave behind.

Desperate and feeling completely out of options, I cried out to God, not just for provision, but for clarity and direction. "Lord, what am I supposed to do? I've tried everything, and I don't see a way out," I whispered through tears. My cry wasn't polished or rehearsed—it was raw, an unfiltered plea from the depths of my soul. And while His answer didn't come immediately in the way I expected, it was unmistakable: "Trust Me."

At first, I didn't know how to act on those words. Trusting God sounded simple in theory, but in practice, it required a level of surrender that felt too challenging. Yet, with nothing to lose and everything to gain, I decided to take a leap of faith. I began applying for jobs I thought were out of my league— positions that seemed reserved for people with more education, more experience, and more connections than I had. I sought out opportunities that intimidated me, knowing that the alternative—staying stuck in fear—was no longer an option.

And step by step, God began to provide. The doors He opened weren't always the ones I anticipated, but each one was a piece of the puzzle He was assembling in my life. One opportunity led to another, and along the way, He brought people into my life who became sources of guidance and support. Mentors appeared seemingly out of nowhere, offering encouragement and resources I hadn't even known existed. They taught me how to think bigger, to see potential in myself that I had long overlooked.

During this time, I also began to experience change that went beyond financial provision—it was spiritual and emotional renewal. God wasn't just meeting my material needs; He was reshaping my perspective. He reminded me that provision isn't solely about what's in your hands; it's about trusting God, as He holds your future. With each step of faith, I gained a deeper understanding of what it meant to rely on Him—not just for the outcomes, but for the strength to take the next step.

One story stands out vividly. I had applied for a position that seemed far beyond my qualifications. The night before the interview, self-doubt began to creep in. "Why would they hire someone like me? What do I have to offer?" I prayed for courage, and as I walked into the interview room, I felt an unexplainable peace wash over me. Instead of focusing on my perceived shortcomings, I spoke from the heart about my passion for serving others and my determination to create a better life for my daughter. To my astonishment, I was offered the job on the spot.

That job was a catalyst for further growth. It provided financial stability for my daughter and me, but more importantly, it reaffirmed the power of trusting God and stepping out in faith. The experience taught me that God's provision often exceeds our expectations, but it requires us to take the first step, even when the ground beneath us feels shaky.

As I look back on that season of transformation, I see how God used those moments of desperation to refine me, to draw me closer to Him, and to prepare me for the work He had in store. The empty fridge and overdue rent notice were not the end of my story—they were the beginning of a new chapter, one filled with hope, resilience, and unwavering trust in a God who provides.

YIELDING TO GOD'S PLAN

Yielding to God's plan didn't mean sitting back and waiting for life to happen—it meant engaging in active obedience, even when the steps I was called to take seemed overwhelming or illogical. Yielding required me to listen for God's voice amidst the noise of my doubts, fears, and the opinions of others. It was about moving forward with faith, trusting that God's plan was better than anything I could devise for myself, even when the path ahead seemed unclear.

One of the most defining moments of yielding came when I felt a strong call to go back to school. At the time, it seemed impossible. I was already stretched thin as a single mother, balancing work and parenting, and the thought of adding school into the mix felt overwhelming. I had no idea how I would juggle it all—financially, logistically, or emotionally. But as much as the practicalities seemed like insurmountable obstacles, the pull to move forward was undeniable. Deep down, I knew that if God was calling me to this path, He would make a way.

And He did.

At first, the way wasn't clear. There were no immediate signs or miraculous breakthroughs, just a quiet assurance that I needed to take the first step. Enrolling in school felt like stepping into uncharted territory, but with each class I attended, each assignment I completed, I saw God's hand at work. He provided resources in unexpected ways, surrounded me with a community of support, and gave me the strength to persevere on days when I felt like giving up.

Yielding was about the small, everyday choices to trust and obey. It was in the moments when I wanted to cling to what felt comfortable, but chose instead to step out in faith. It was in saying yes to opportunities that seemed beyond my capacity, believing that God wouldn't bring me to a place without equipping me to succeed. Each act of obeying God's purpose for my life, no matter how small, became a brick in the foundation of the new legacy I was building—a legacy free from the curses that had held my family captive for generations.

With every decision to follow God's lead, I could feel the chains loosening. The fear that had once paralyzed me like quick sand began to dissipate, replaced by a growing sense of confidence in myself and God's promises. I realized that obedience was about aligning myself with a purpose that was far greater than anything I could have envisioned. It was about trusting that God's perspective was infinitely larger than mine and that He saw the entire picture while I could only see a fragment.

One of the greatest lessons I learned during this time was that obedience is often the key to unlocking blessings we didn't even know were waiting for us. By saying yes to God's plan, I found doors opening that I could never have forced open on my own. Opportunities that seemed unattainable became accessible. Relationships that felt irreparably broken began to heal. And most importantly, I began to see the ripple effects me walking in forgiveness and healing changed the trajectory of my house.

Each step of yielding, whether it was enrolling in school, making sacrifices to prioritize my daughter, or confronting painful patterns in my own life, became a declaration of faith. It was my way of saying, "I trust You, God, even when I don't understand. I trust You, even when it's hard. I trust You, because Your plan is better than mine." And through that trust, I witnessed the incredible truth that God's plans are indeed for our good, and that obedience is the pathway to breaking free and stepping into the fullness of His purpose for our lives.

A MOMENT OF BREAKTHROUGH

There are moments in life so transformative that they feel like the earth beneath you shifts, ushering in a new season of growth, freedom, and opportunities to thrive. For me, one of those moments came in the quiet of a church service, during a time of intense prayer. I had been carrying the weight of a relationship that had left me deeply wounded. The pain, betrayal, and resentment from that relationship had taken root in my heart, festering in ways that affected not just my emotional state, but also my spirit. I thought holding on to that anger would protect me, acting as a shield against further hurt. But in reality, it had become a prison—one I didn't even realize I was locked in.

As I knelt in prayer, I felt God's gentle urging, His voice clear in my heart: "Forgive." At first, I resisted. Forgiveness felt impossible, even undeserved. How could I let go of the hurt someone else had caused? What would it mean to release the anger that, in many ways, had become part of my identity? It felt safer to hold on to my pain, to use it as proof that I had been wronged. But as I wrestled with these thoughts, a wave of clarity came over me. God wasn't asking me to condone what had happened or to excuse the harm that had been done. He was asking me to release myself from the chains of bitterness that were keeping me bound.

I sat there, tears streaming down my face, fighting an internal battle. My mind wanted to cling to the anger, but my heart longed for freedom. Finally, I whispered a simple prayer: "I forgive." And in that moment, something shifted. It was as though a weight I hadn't even fully understood was lifted from my shoulders. The pain didn't vanish instantly, but its grip on me loosened. I could feel the beginnings of healing, the space in my heart opening up for peace to take root.

That act of forgiveness wasn't just about releasing the person who had hurt me—it was about releasing myself. It was about reclaiming the parts of my soul that had been overshadowed by frustration and grief. For the first time, I realized that forgiveness wasn't a gift to the other person; it was a gift to myself. It was a declaration that my healing was more important than my hurt, that my future was more valuable than my past.

This breakthrough moment became a defining lesson in my journey to break generational curses. It reminded me that true freedom starts from within. Generational curses often manifest as external struggles—poverty, broken relationships, or cycles of dysfunction—but at their core, they are rooted in the internal wounds we carry. To break those curses, we must confront the pain that keeps them alive and choose to heal, even when it's hard.

Forgiveness taught me the power of surrender. It showed me that letting go is not a sign of weakness, but of incredible strength. It allowed me to see the people who had hurt me through a lens of grace, understanding that they, too, were shaped by their own wounds and struggles. And in that grace, I found compassion—not just for them, but for myself.

That moment in church wasn't the end of my journey, but it was a turning point. It set me on a path of intentional healing, teaching me that breaking generational curses requires more than external change. It demands that we do the hard, messy work of mending our internal wounds, confronting the pain we've avoided, and allowing God's love to transform us from the inside out.

Each time I reflect on that day, I am reminded of this truth: forgiveness isn't about what we lose—it's about what we gain. It's about stepping into the freedom, peace, and healing that God has always intended for us. That moment wasn't just an emotional release; it was a spiritual breakthrough that testified to the power of obedience and the transformative work of grace in my life.

THE RIPPLE EFFECT

The choices we make in life don't just impact us—they reverberate through the lives of those around us, shaping futures we may never fully see. As I walked the path of breaking generational curses, I began to witness the ripple effects of my decisions. Every act of faith, every step toward healing, and every moment of choosing love over fear created waves that extended beyond me, touching my daughter and, eventually, those in our broader community.

For my daughter, the impact was significant. She grew up in an environment that felt radically different from the one I had known. Where I had experienced chaos, she found stability. Where I had once absorbed fear, she was surrounded by faith. She watched as I navigated life's trials—not with bitterness or despair, but with resilience, hope, and trust in God's plan. I saw her carry these lessons into her own life, choosing hope and determination because she had seen what they could accomplish. The love and consistency I poured into her became a foundation she could stand on, a new legacy that replaced the fractures of the past.

But the ripple effect didn't stop with her. As I leaned into God's purpose for my life and embraced healing, I found that my story inspired others. Whether it was friends, family members, or people in my community, they saw the transformation in my life and began to believe that change was possible for them, too. Conversations shifted from complaints about the weight of generational curses to discussions about how to break free from them. My willingness to step into the hard work of healing created space for others to imagine what healing could look like in their own lives.

Breaking generational curses is an ongoing, lifelong commitment. It requires a daily choice to grow, to let go of old patterns, and to replace them with new habits rooted in faith, love, and resilience. It's deciding, again and again, to live unapologetically free—not just for your own benefit, but for the generations that follow. Each day, I recommitted to being intentional with my actions, aware that every choice I made had the potential to shape the legacy I lived and desired to leave behind.

There were moments when the weight of this responsibility felt overwhelming. The scars of the past didn't simply vanish because I decided to heal; they lingered, demanding attention and effort. But in those moments, I remembered why I was doing this work. I thought of my daughter and the life I wanted her to live. I thought of the people in my community who needed to see that transformation was possible. Most importantly, I thought of the faithfulness of God, who had walked with me every step of the way, equipping me with the strength to keep moving forward.

One of the most humbling realizations was that breaking generational curses was about building a future that reflected God's promises. It wasn't enough to simply stop the cycle of pain and dysfunction; I wanted to replace it with a legacy of joy, love, and faith. I wanted to plant seeds that would grow into something beautiful, something that would bear fruit for years to come.

The process is far from easy, but it is always worth it. Each step forward—no matter how small—creates ripples that expand outward, touching lives in ways we may never fully understand or know is taking place. It's a reminder that healing is not just personal; it's generational. It's a gift we give to ourselves, to those we love, and to the world around us.

Today, I see those ripples continuing to spread. I see it in the strength and compassion of my daughter, who is now building her own life with the tools I worked so hard to give her. I see it in the people who reach out to share how my story has inspired them to start their own journey of healing. And I see it in the lives I inspire with the work I do, in quiet moments of reflection, when I look back on how far we've come. I have to thank God for His faithfulness.

Breaking generational curses is about creating a legacy of hope, healing, purpose, and faith that will echo for generations to come. And that, more than anything, makes every sacrifice, every struggle, and every act of obedience worth it.

A NEW LEGACY

Today, I stand as the cycle breaker and living proof that generational curses can be broken. The patterns of dysfunction, pain, and limitation that once defined my family's history have been replaced with hope, love, healing, growth, and resilience. This transformation did not come easily; it was born out of faith and willingness to surrender everything I thought I knew in exchange for everything God promised. And while the journey is far from over, the cycles that once held us captive have been disrupted, their power diminished. For this, I am profoundly and humbly grateful.

Breaking these curses has been about building something new. A new legacy, rooted in faith and resilience, now serves as the foundation for my family and for the generations to come. This legacy is one where love replaces bitterness, where strength overcomes fear, and where faith lights the pathway forward even in the darkest moments. It's a legacy that acknowledges the pain of the past, but refuses to let that pain dictate the future.

This chapter of my life is about building a foundation for something greater. Each choice I made to trust God, to obey His direction, and to surrender my own limited understanding was a brick in that foundation. I learned that God's plan is not just about healing the wounds we carry—it's about equipping us to thrive, to become beacons of hope for others, and to show what is possible when we trust.

There were moments when the sacrifices felt overwhelming, when the weight of rewriting my family's story seemed too heavy to bear. But as I look back, I see not just the struggles, but the victories that have shaped me into the woman I am today. I see the strength that was forged in the fire of adversity. I see the resilience that came from leaning into God's plan, even when it was unclear. And I see the evidence of His faithfulness in every step of my journey.

This new legacy isn't just for me—it's for my daughter, for her children, and for every generation that comes after us. It's for the families I've been able to inspire and for the communities I've been called to serve. It's a reminder that no matter how entrenched the cycles of dysfunction may seem, they can be broken. And when they are, the ripple effects of healing and hope can transform not just one life, but many.

As I stand here today, I am filled with gratitude—for the struggles that taught me resilience, for the faith that sustained me, and for the hope that keeps me moving forward. God's promises and His plans are always bigger than our pain. This journey has not only changed my life; it has redefined what is possible for my family and for anyone willing to trust God's plan.

The work isn't done, but the foundation is set. A new legacy has begun, one that honors the struggles of the past while embracing the possibilities of the future. And as I continue to walk this path, I am reminded daily that His grace is sufficient, His unconditional love is unending, and His promises are always worth every sacrifice. For this, I am not just grateful—I am transformed.

SELF-AWARENESS AND REFLECTION

1. *Family Patterns Inventory:* Reflect on your family history. What patterns, beliefs, or behaviors do you see repeating across generations? How have they impacted your life?

_____

_____

_____

_____

_____

_____

_____

_____

_____

_____

_____

2. *Your Chains:* Identify at least one "chain" or cycle you feel bound by. What steps can you take to begin breaking free from it?

_____

_____

_____

_____

_____

_____

_____

_____

_____

_____

_____

_____

3. *Forgiveness Reflection:* Who or what do you need to forgive in order to move forward? Write a letter (even if you don't send it) expressing your feelings and releasing the hurt.

_____
_____
_____
_____
_____
_____
_____
_____
_____
_____
_____

4. *Legacy Vision:* Imagine the legacy you want to leave behind. What values, habits, or lessons do you want to pass down to the next generation?

_____
_____
_____
_____
_____
_____
_____
_____
_____
_____
_____

5. Inner Healing: Think about a moment when you felt unworthy or burdened by past mistakes. How can you show yourself grace and take a step toward healing?

_____

_____

_____

_____

_____

_____

_____

_____

_____

_____

TIPS FOR BREAKING GENERATIONAL CURSES

- *Identify the Patterns:* Acknowledge the cycles of dysfunction in your family history. Awareness is the first step toward change.

- *Seek Help:* Don't be afraid to seek professional counseling, pastoral support, or a trusted mentor to help you navigate the process of breaking curses.

- *Build New Habits:* Replace unhealthy behaviors with new routines and practices that align with your values and goals.

- *Practice Forgiveness:* Release bitterness and resentment through the act of forgiveness. It frees you more than it frees the other person.

- *Celebrate Progress:* Breaking generational curses is hard work. Celebrate even the smallest victories along the way.

How can you implement the aforementioned tips in your daily life?

_____

_____

_____

_____

_____

_____

_____

_____

_____

_____

_____

_____

_____

_____

QUOTES TO INSPIRE

" *"He heals the brokenhearted and binds up their wounds."*
   – Psalm 147:3

" *"Generational curses are real, but so is generational healing. Be the one who chooses to heal." – Unknown*

" *"Forgiveness is not about forgetting. It is about letting go of another person's throat." – William Paul Young*

After reflecting on these quotes, journal your thoughts below.

_____

_____

_____

_____

_____

_____

_____

_____

_____

_____

_____

_____

_____

_____

_____

_____

_____

_____

_____

_____

_____

_____

_____

_____

_____

_____

_____

_____

_____

_____

_____

_____

CHAPTER SIX
Mind Over Matter

Success often begins with a shift in perspective. For me, it wasn't just about changing my circumstances; it was about changing the way I thought. The journey from survival to thriving required me to confront limiting beliefs, break free from ingrained patterns, and embrace a mindset that fostered growth, resilience, and hope. The transformative power of a growth mindset and the tools I relied on to overcome mental barriers that threatened to hold me back are central to this journey.

FIXED VS. GROWTH MINDSET

A fixed mindset is the belief that abilities and intelligence are static, that what you're born with is all you'll ever have. In this mindset, failure is seen as a reflection of your limitations, and challenges are often avoided out of fear of exposing inadequacies. On the other hand, a growth mindset embraces the idea that abilities can be developed through hard work, persistence, and learning. Here, challenges become opportunities, and failure is viewed as a step closer to growth.

Growing up in the hood, I didn't know what a growth mindset

was, let alone how to cultivate one. What I did know was survival: how to navigate the complexities of my environment, avoid pitfalls, and make it through each day. There wasn't room for lofty aspirations when survival required immediate focus. Dreams felt more like fantasies—unrealistic goals reserved for people with privilege, stability, or access to opportunities I couldn't imagine.

The narrative around me reinforced this fixed mindset. I'd hear phrases like, "People like us don't succeed," or "This is just how life is." These messages painted a picture of limitation, convincing me that there was an invisible ceiling on what I could achieve. Success stories were rare and often seemed unattainable— their protagonists appearing more like outliers than evidence of possibility. Scarcity didn't just affect our finances; it affected our hope, opportunity, and belief in a better future.

For a long time, I absorbed this mindset as truth. I believed I wasn't meant for more, that the circumstances of my upbringing were my destiny. When I struggled in school or faced rejection, it felt like confirmation of those limitations, as though the world was reinforcing that I wasn't enough.

But something began to shift throughout my educational journey. It wasn't a single moment of revelation, but rather a series of small cracks in the wall of my beliefs. Education became a window into a world I hadn't seen before—a world where hard work and perseverance could lead to holistic success. I started to meet people who had overcome similar obstacles, and their stories planted seeds of possibility within me. Maybe I could be more. Maybe success wasn't just for "them."

Faith also played a pivotal role in this shift. I began to lean into God, who spoke of purpose, potential, and a plan greater than anything I could imagine. Faith taught me that my circumstances didn't have to define my future, and that failure wasn't the end—it was just a part of the process. This belief was liberating. It gave me permission to hope, to dream, and to try.

As I continued on this path, I realized that the limitations I'd accepted weren't facts; they were perceptions shaped by my environment. I learned that I could challenge those beliefs, replace them with new ones, and begin to build a life defined not by where I came from, but by where I wanted to go. Education and faith became my tools for breaking the cycle of scarcity, both in my thinking and in my life. They helped me shift from seeing challenges as roadblocks to viewing them as opportunities for growth. And in doing so, they opened the door to a future I had once thought was out of reach.

TRANSFORMATIVE MINDSET MOMENTS

There are moments in life that serve as turning points—when you're faced with a choice: to stay in the comfort of what you know or to step into the unknown and risk failure. These moments are the catalysts for transformation, and for me, they marked the beginnings of a growth mindset.

One of the most defining moments came during my academic journey. I had always struggled with feelings of inadequacy, especially when it came to writing. Academic standards felt like towering walls I couldn't climb. I told myself stories like, "You're not a good writer" or "You don't belong here." These thoughts weren't just doubts—they were barriers that made me question if it was worth trying.

But deep down, there was a flicker of determination. I knew that if I wanted to succeed, I couldn't let my fears win. Instead of giving up, I decided to lean into the discomfort. I began seeking out resources: attending writing workshops, consulting with tutors, and asking professors for feedback. At first, the progress felt painstakingly slow, but with each draft I improved, and with each revision, my confidence grew.

I remember the moment I received a paper back with a note from a professor that read, "Great improvement—keep going." It was a simple comment, but it meant everything to me. It was proof that growth was possible. Each small success began to chip away at the narrative I had internalized—that I wasn't "smart enough." Slowly, but surely, I replaced it with a new story: I am capable, and I can learn.

Another transformative moment came during a job application process. I had my eye on a position that felt like a perfect fit for my goals and skills. But as I prepared my application, the familiar voices of self-doubt crept in: "You're not qualified." "You're going to embarrass yourself." "Why bother trying?"

I wrestled with these thoughts, teetering on the edge of walking away entirely. But then, I decided to take a different approach. Instead of focusing on the potential rejection, I reframed the experience as an opportunity to grow. Even if I didn't get the job, I told myself, I would gain valuable experience from the application process. I could learn how to tailor my resume, improve my interviewing skills, and refine my approach for the next opportunity.

With this shift in perspective, I felt the fear begin to loosen its grip. I submitted my application, and to my surprise, I was called for an interview. Though I didn't get that particular position, the experience was invaluable. I walked away with insights I carried into future applications—insights that ultimately helped me land a role that was even better suited for me.

What these moments taught me was that a growth mindset isn't about eliminating fear or self-doubt—it's about changing the way you respond to them. It's about seeing failure not as a reflection of your worth, but as a step in the process of becoming better. Each time I leaned into discomfort, whether in academics or the job market, I grew stronger, more confident, and more resilient.

These shifts weren't easy. They required intentional effort, patience, and the willingness to be vulnerable. But each small victory proved to me that growth is possible, even in the face of doubt. Over time, I learned to trust the process, to believe in my ability to learn, and to embrace the challenges that once felt insurmountable. These moments became the foundation for a mindset that would carry me through future obstacles, showing me that the potential for growth is always within reach.

MENTAL ROADBLOCKS

The journey toward a growth mindset was anything, but simple. Along the way, I encountered numerous mental roadblocks that threatened to derail my progress. These obstacles were deeply ingrained beliefs and emotional burdens that I had carried for much of my life. Overcoming them required intentional effort, faith, and resilience.

One of the most persistent challenges I faced was impostor syndrome—the overwhelming belief that I was a fraud, that my achievements were mere flukes, and that at any moment, someone would expose me as unworthy of the spaces I had worked so hard to enter. This feeling wasn't tied to reality, but to a narrative I had absorbed growing up, one that whispered, "You don't belong here."

Even as I accomplished things I had once thought impossible—getting into college, excelling in academics, landing jobs—I couldn't shake the nagging sense that I didn't deserve any of it. Every achievement felt like luck rather than hard-earned success, and I constantly feared that others would see through my façade. Impostor syndrome became a relentless companion, one that often made me question my capabilities.

Fear of failure was another formidable roadblock. The idea of falling short felt like confirmation of every doubt I'd ever had about myself. I worried that failing would not only expose my inadequacies, but also prove that I wasn't capable of breaking free from the cycles of limitation I had grown up in. This fear became paralyzing at times, making me hesitate to take risks or pursue opportunities that could propel me forward.

The fear wasn't just about external judgment—it was also internal. I didn't want to let myself down. Failure felt like a reflection of my worth, as though falling short would mean that I was fundamentally flawed or destined for mediocrity.

Beneath the impostor syndrome and fear of failure lay a deeper sense of inadequacy tied to the constant pressure for code switching. It wasn't just that I doubted my abilities; I questioned my inherent worth. Growing up in an environment where survival often took precedence over self-worth, I had internalized the idea that I wasn't enough—not smart enough, not talented enough, not deserving enough, which came from word curses spoken over me.

This belief shaped the way I saw myself and the world around me. Opportunities felt out of reach, not because they were impossible, but because I didn't believe I had the right to pursue them. I second-guessed my every decision, convinced that I was incapable of making the "right" choices. This sense of inadequacy became a self-fulfilling cycle, where my own doubts kept me from fully stepping into my potential.

These mental roadblocks affected my emotional and spiritual health, as well. They tied into wounds from my past, moments when I had been overlooked, underestimated, or dismissed. The feelings of unworthiness were reinforced by external circumstances, but rooted in internal beliefs. Spiritually, I struggled to reconcile my faith with my doubts, wondering how I could truly trust in God's plan for me when I didn't feel worthy of it.

At times, these roadblocks felt as though they were permanent fixtures in my life. But what I came to realize was that they were challenges to be faced, not truths to be accepted. Overcoming them required a deep commitment to self-reflection, faith, and the gradual process of rewriting the narratives I had carried for so long.

Through intentional work, I began to dismantle the mental, emotional, spiritual, systemic barriers that held me back. I learned that while impostor syndrome, fear of failure, and inadequacy might still whisper their lies, they didn't have to define me. With every step forward, I proved to myself that I was capable of growth and deserving of the success and fulfillment I had worked so hard to achieve.

PRACTICAL STRATEGIES FOR MINDSET SHIFTS

Overcoming the mental roadblocks that threatened to derail my journey required intentional effort and the adoption of practical strategies to reframe my thinking. These tools didn't just help me survive; they allowed me to thrive, shifting my mindset from one of limitation to one of endless possibilities.

Affirmations became a cornerstone of my daily routine. Each morning, I intentionally spoke life into my situation with phrases like, "I am capable," "I am worthy," "I am brave, bold, beautiful," and "God's plan for me is greater than my fear." These simple yet powerful statements helped counteract the negativity that often felt overwhelming. By consistently repeating these affirmations, I began to internalize the truth of my potential and shift my self-perception.

Journaling became another transformative practice. Writing offered me a space to reflect, release, process my emotions, and gain clarity. By putting my thoughts on paper, I was able to identify patterns in my thinking, challenge the false beliefs that held me back, and celebrating even the smallest victories. For me, journaling was about creating a narrative of growth and resilience that I could return to whenever doubt threatened to creep in.

Faith practices, including prayer and meditation, served as my anchor during moments of uncertainty. Whenever fear or doubt loomed large, I turned to God for guidance and reassurance. These quiet moments of communion with Him reminded me that I wasn't alone in my journey and that there was a greater plan unfolding, even when I couldn't yet see it.

Building a supportive and caring community was equally transformative. I surrounded myself with people who believed in me and challenged me to grow. Mentors, friends, and faith leaders became invaluable sources of encouragement and accountability.

Their insights and support reinforced the belief that I could rise above my circumstances and achieve more than I had ever imagined.

Reframing failure was perhaps one of the most significant mindset shifts I made. Instead of viewing setbacks as definitive endings, I began to see them as opportunities to learn, adjust, and try again. This shift in perspective allowed me to approach challenges with curiosity and resilience rather than fear. Failure no longer felt like a reflection of my inadequacy, but rather a natural part of the journey toward success.

Together, these strategies formed a framework that empowered me to navigate life's challenges with strength and determination. They became tools not only for overcoming obstacles, but for transforming my entire outlook on what was possible for my life.

THE SHIFT FROM SURVIVAL TO THRIVING

Transitioning from survival mode to a mindset focused on success was neither straightforward nor instantaneous—it was a journey that required intentional growth and persistent effort. Survival mode had been my default setting for so long, teaching me how to endure in the face of adversity. It sharpened my ability to navigate crises, solve problems on the fly, and make sacrifices to meet immediate needs. However, living in survival mode came with its limitations. It kept my focus narrow, centered solely on getting through the day or the week, leaving little room for dreams, goals, or long-term planning. Survival was about getting by, but success demanded that I imagine more.

Success required a shift in perspective—one that allowed me to think beyond the immediate struggles and embrace the possibility of a brighter future. It wasn't just about having enough to pay the bills or put food on the table; it was about creating a life of abundance, stability, and purpose. This shift meant breaking free from the scarcity mindset that had been ingrained in me from years of struggle. I had to retrain my thinking to believe that I deserved success and that it was within my reach.

The transition also demanded vision and planning—two skills that weren't prioritized in survival mode. In survival, there's no time to plan for tomorrow when today's needs feel so pressing. But moving toward success required me to step back, look at the bigger picture, and set clear goals for my future. This wasn't easy; it involved risk, vulnerability, and the willingness to hope for things I couldn't yet see. I had to learn how to dream again—something I had abandoned during the darkest moments of survival.

Believing in possibilities that weren't yet visible was perhaps the hardest part of the transition. Success required faith— in God, myself, and the path He was leading me on. It required me to trust that the sacrifices I was making and the seeds I was planting would one day bear fruit. It meant taking bold steps, like going back to school, pursuing opportunities outside my comfort zone, and rejecting the limiting beliefs that told me I was aiming too high.

Survival had taught me resilience, but success taught me vision. It taught me to look beyond the struggles of today and build a foundation for the future. This shift didn't mean forgetting the lessons of survival—in fact, those lessons became the building blocks of my success. But it meant learning to live with purpose, embracing growth, and trusting that the life I had always dreamed of was possible.

The greatest battles we face are often fought and won within the mind. Shifting from a fixed mindset to a growth mindset wasn't merely an exercise in personal development; it was an act of liberation—breaking free from the chains of limiting beliefs that had been handed down through generations. It was about reclaiming the power to define my own narrative and, in doing so, laying the groundwork for a brighter future for myself and my family.

Adopting a growth mindset meant confronting deeply ingrained fears, doubts, and the scars left by past experiences. It required me to unlearn the idea that my worth was tethered to my circumstances and replace it with the belief that my potential was limitless. Each decision to choose growth over stagnation became a step toward rewriting a legacy—proving that our environment does not have the final say in our destiny.

This journey was fueled by faith, determination, and the tools I cultivated along the way. Faith gave me the courage to dream and the strength to persevere. Determination pushed me to keep going, even when the road ahead felt uncertain. And the practical strategies I embraced—affirmations, journaling, prayer, seeking community, and reframing failure—became lifelines, guiding me through moments of doubt and fear.

Perhaps the most significant realization was that this transformation wasn't just about me. Every mindset shift, every step forward, was an investment in a future where my family and those around me could see what was possible. It was about breaking cycles of limitation and inspiring others to believe in their own potential for growth and change.

Mind over matter became more than a catchy saying; it became a way of life. It taught me that while external challenges may feel overwhelming, the true battleground is within. By choosing faith over fear, growth over comfort, and resilience over resignation, I discovered that transformation is always attainable. It's not easy, but it's worth every moment of effort. This became the foundation for a life defined not by circumstances, but by the boundless possibilities of the mind.

SELF-AWARENESS AND REFLECTION

1. Mindset Audit: Reflect on a current challenge in your life. Are you approaching it with a fixed mindset or a growth mindset? What would it look like to reframe this challenge as a growth opportunity?

_____
_____
_____
_____
_____
_____
_____
_____
_____
_____

2. Limiting Beliefs: Write down three beliefs you have about yourself that might be holding you back. For each one, ask: Is this belief abso-lutely true? What evidence do I have that contradicts it?

_____
_____
_____
_____
_____
_____
_____
_____
_____
_____
_____

3. Visualize Your Success: Imagine your life five years from now. What goals have you achieved? How has your mindset contributed to your success? Write a journal entry as if you are living that future life.

_____

_____

_____

_____

_____

_____

_____

_____

_____

_____

_____

4. Failure Reflection: Think about a recent failure or setback. What did you learn from the experience? How can you use this lesson to approach future challenges differently?

_____

_____

_____

_____

_____

_____

_____

_____

_____

_____

_____

_____

5. Support Network: Who in your life encourages a growth mindset? Are there people you need to distance yourself from or others you should lean into more?

_____

_____

_____

_____

_____

_____

_____

_____

_____

_____

_____

_____

TIPS FOR CULTIVATING A GROWTH MINDSET

- *Practice Gratitude:* Each day, write down three things you're grateful for, focusing on opportunities to learn and grow.

- *Seek Feedback:* Actively ask for feedback from trusted mentors or peers and use it to improve rather than as a measure of your worth.

- *Set Process-Oriented Goals:* Instead of focusing solely on outcomes, create goals that reward effort and improvement. For example, aim to "write for 30 minutes every day" rather than "finish a perfect paper."

- *Challenge Your Comfort Zone:* Take small steps daily to do something that scares you or feels difficult. Growth lives on the edge of your comfort zone.

How can you implement the aforementioned tips in your daily life?

_____

_____

_____

_____

_____

_____

_____

_____

_____

_____

_____

_____

_____

_____

_____

_____

QUOTES TO INSPIRE

Do not be conformed to this world, but be transformed by the renewal of your mind. – Romans 12:2

Whether you think you can or think you can't, you're right. – Henry Ford

Your greatest battles are won in your mind. – Unknown

After reflecting on these quotes, journal your thoughts below.

_____

_____

_____

_____

_____

_____

_____

_____

_____

_____

_____

_____

_____

_____

_____

_____

_____

_____

_____

_____

_____

_____

_____

_____

_____

_____

_____

_____

_____

Acknowledgments

> "Unapologetically free is the destination with the goal of being bold, brave, brilliant, and building beyond barriers with a standard of excellence so you can excel. Even when the cares of life detour you, know that you are still on track, so prepare for the reroute. - Dr. Shatoya Black

*   *   *

It's important to acknowledge that changes often occur no matter what stage of life you are in. These times of change can be challenging to navigate, requiring you to avoid getting stuck and maintain the discipline needed to thrive. During these times, I learned that the power of perspective is key, tragedy can be turned into triumph, and there is strength in finding your voice through self-advocacy. This inspired my book *From Hood to Hooded*™, which I hope will provide a different perspective.

The first honor goes to God for His instruction, purpose, and for ordering my steps to become the multifaceted woman of power, virtue, integrity, and innovative visionary leader I am today. He allowed me to develop the understanding that all things work together for my good as I took my journey *from hood to hooded*™.

I hope every person who reads this book and engages with its interactive experience feels inspired and empowered to move forward. This book aims to show how important your voice is to your overall well-being and to affirm that you are more than enough. I also hope readers will pay it forward by blessing someone they know with a copy, so they too can be liberated and shifted in their perspective, embarking on a journey of triumph and holistic success.

Thank you to my daughter for being the reason I desired to thrive and become the best version of myself. Being a cycle-breaker was no simple task and required a commitment to self-awareness and self-leadership to change learned behaviors. You have been my greatest example and cheerleader during times when I navigated alone. The fruit of my daughter's life and those I have impacted is a living example of the manifestation of cycles and barriers being broken.

Thank you to my mom for not aborting me as a teen parent and for everything you sacrificed to ensure we had the best with less. *Thank you to my father* for the efforts made to connect and build relationships, even without the right tools, abilities, and examples to do so. My journey through life has helped me appreciate and understand that my parents did their best as young parents themselves.

Thank you to my grandmother, who made the biggest silent sacrifices to help others in their times of need as part of their village, even when her own needs were neglected. Thank you, Grandma, for being the pillar of our family and teaching us what it means to be strong through adversity.

Thank you to those from my childhood in the hood who served as my village, helping me learn "street smarts" and being examples of overcomers.

Thank you to my village in college at Northern Illinois University, who assisted me in countless ways during my journey to complete college.

Thank you to the TRIO Association for helping me grow into the professional I am today and for the continued impact you have on first-generation college students from low socioeconomic backgrounds.

Thank you to all the people who served as my community of care and agents of C.H.A.N.G.E.™ in my life, providing me with wisdom, insight, resources, and opportunities to grow.

Finally, thank you to Dr. LaVerne Gyant, my Chair, and Dr. Coates, who were instrumental in helping me complete my doctorate at Northern Illinois University and finish strong.

About the Author

Dr. Shatoya Black is the CEO and Founder of Legacy Life Navigator LLC, which focuses on providing guidance and strategies for success. She is the past president of the Illinois TRIO Association, Project Director for Student Support Services (SSS) at Illinois State University, and a proud alumna of TRIO SSS at Northern Illinois University. Black was born and raised on the south side of Chicago and is the oldest of fourteen siblings. Her journey to college began without a place to call home, but she was offered a place to stay in DeKalb, Illinois, where she completed her degrees at Northern Illinois University, culminating in a doctorate in education.

She currently plays a strategically innovative role in developing initiatives that impact the holistic success of first-generation students and professionals, both personally and academically. With over fifteen years of experience, Dr. Black has dedicated her career to helping students navigate critical transition points in their lives.

Dr. Black has cultivated spaces that focus on closing the opportunity gap, building community, and addressing deficit perspectives and language to shift the narrative of first-generation students to an asset-based approach. She takes a holistic approach to success by highlighting the social and cultural capital students bring to the college environment. She has created intentional programming to elevate and amplify the voices of first-generation students' lived experiences.

Dr. Black has developed initiatives such as an inaugural campus-wide first-generation celebration, identity and career pathway development programs, student affinity groups, the First-Generation Triumph Podcast, direct-touch persistence, retention, and completion programs, First-Gen Fridays, financial enrichment programs, course development, innovative practical and experiential learning experiences, and language that liberates.

She has also implemented community impact projects that cultivate the 5A's of career development and has created a Legacy framework to guide students and professionals in identifying and navigating holistic success. Additionally, she founded the Unique I.M.P.A.C.T.™ initiative, which has been active for 15 years, and the C.H.A.N.G.E.™ initiative to inspire and empower others to embrace the change found within challenges.

Dr. Black draws on the impactful mentorship she received from TRIO association leaders during her own journey of growth and development to provide that same level of understanding and support to others as lifelong learners. She is an empowerment agent who believes that first-generation students and professionals face significant challenges in achieving their life goals without equitable opportunities. When there is a gap in opportunity, the ability to succeed often feels out of reach. Closing this gap requires identifying and addressing the factors keeping it open.

For more information or to get in contact with Shatoya,
please scan the QR code below.